THE MICROWAVE COOKBOOK

THE MICROWAVE COOKBOOK

ANNEMARIE ROSIER

NEW YORK

First published in USA 1986
by Exeter Books
Distributed by Bookthrift
Exeter is a trademark of Bookthrift Marketing, Inc.
Bookthrift is a registered trademark of Bookthrift Marketing, Inc.
New York, New York

ISBN 0-671-07750-3

Printed in Portugal

Acknowledgements

Photography by Chris Crofton
Food prepared by Annemarie Rosier
Stylist Pip Kelly

Line drawings by Paul Saunders

The author and publisher would like to thank the following companies for sponsoring photographs:

Corning Microwave Ware **and** Pyrex Classics Bakeware (page 33); Grand Marnier (page 61); Thorpac Group plc (page 53) **and** Toshiba (UK) Ltd (page 37).

CONTENTS

Notes

It is important to follow the metric, imperial **or** American measures when using the recipes in this book. Do not use a combination of measures.

American terminology is indicated by the use of brackets. For 'microwave cooker', however, read 'microwave oven'.

American measures which follow metric and imperial measures within the recipe methods are preceded by the term 'US'.

All recipes serve four people, unless otherwise specified.

All spoon measures are level.

All recipes have been tested on a standard 650 watt microwave cooker using three power levels:

HIGH/100%   MEDIUM/50%   DEFROST/25%

Check with instruction book or manufacturer as to equivalent levels on other cookers, and adjust the timings as necessary.

If using a combination cooker, browning and grilling can be carried out in the cooker itself rather than separately. Check with instruction book or manufacturer if in doubt.

All recipe timings are approximate, depending on the cooker used.

Sizes of cookware used within recipes, unless otherwise specified:

	Minimum	Maximum
Small	600ml/1 pint/2½ US cups	1.5 litres/2½ pints/1¼ US quarts
Medium	1.5 litres/2½ pints/1¼ US quarts	2.1 litres/3½ pints/1¾ US quarts
Large	2.1 litres/3½ pints/1¾ US quarts	3.6 litres/6 pints/3 US quarts
Jug (Measuring cup)	1 litre/1¾ pints/4½ US cups	

Important
If you have a pacemaker, check with your doctor before purchasing a microwave cooker.

INTRODUCTION

Since the appearance of the first domestic microwave cookers, the market has grown exceptionally fast. This would not have happened if the cooking results had not matched the other advantages. Today's microwave cookers will cook sixty to ninety per cent of everyday food, and can produce a wide variety of items from a delicate sauce to a warming casserole with results which will satisfy the most critical connoisseur. All of this is achieved in far less time than by conventional methods, and with none of the loss of moisture or flavour that is often associated with fast cooking.

Consequently, people who enjoy cooking will find that their repertoire will expand rapidly. For those who dislike cooking, meals of a high standard can be produced with very little work.

Additionally, there are the invaluable bonuses of defrosting and re-heating within minutes, thereby considerably shortening the time spent planning meals and cooking food.

The microwave cooker has many other benefits to the users, whether they are young, old, live-aloners or families. Running costs are low, as the average microwave cooker uses only 1.2kw of electricity per hour. In that time, a Sunday lunch can be cooked, and a cake baked. The cooker automatically switches off at the end of the cooking time, and no energy is wasted by having to pre-heat it.

There is less washing up as food can often be served from the cooking container. The cookware, too, remains cleaner as food is not baked on to it.

Very little steam and cooking smells escape from a microwave cooker, so that it is not necessary to keep it near an extractor fan. Additionally, the microwave cooker remains cool when in use—a great advantage in hot weather.

It can, in fact, be placed anywhere there is a suitable point (electrical outlet), whether a dining room or living room during a party, to keep the mulled wine flowing or hot snacks coming. With the aid of an extension lead (cord), it can be used to part cook chicken, ribs, chops and sausages for barbecuing—the perfect answer to the guest who wants a well-done steak!

Many of the recipes in this book are variations on family favourites. Others are new to help you to make more imaginative use of your microwave cooker.

Annemarie Rosier

What's What in Microwave Cookers

When domestic microwave cookers were first launched, it was simpler to choose one, but with so many models now available it can be difficult to decide.

Manufacturers are continually developing additional new features to make the use of microwave cookers more automatic and flexible in their functions.

Most microwave cookers are counter-top models that can be built into work units. Others are part of free-standing cookers, or built-in double oven/grill systems.

The cookers vary in five main ways: size, speed, inclusion of a turntable, controls and additional features.

SIZE

This is important as it relates to the cooking cavity. A small cavity is suitable for a single person or small family as the size of dishes which are suitable is limited. For the large family or for people who entertain, a larger cavity is needed.

SPEED

The speed of the microwave cookers ranges from 500 to 720 watts; the higher the wattage, the faster the food is cooked or heated. The smaller cookers have the lower wattage generally, the larger ones, the higher.

TURNTABLE OR NOT

There is a tray on which the food is placed, on the base of the cooking cavity. This can be either a turntable which automatically rotates when the oven is working, a removable static tray or a sealed-in shelf. At the top of the microwave cooker there is usually a stirrer fan or a direction mode which distributes the waves around the cavity. The turntable, by rotating the food, ensures that it is evenly cooked. In cookers without turntables

some foods, eg cakes, have to be turned by hand during cooking to ensure even rising. There can also be a form of turntable/stirrer underneath the sealed base; this is known as a rotating antennae. Check to see whether the turntable motor connection is removable or not, so that large, oblong or square dishes can be placed in the cooker without touching the sides.

CONTROLS

The actual controls are either knobs to be turned, buttons to be pressed or touch pads.

Switching on the Cooker

This is done either by an on/off switch or by setting the cooker timer. The cooker will not start operating until the time or programme is set, and the start button or pad is pressed.

Start of Cooking Switch

This sometimes lights up to show the cooker is working, or there may be a separate indicator. At the end of the cooking time, the light switches off, and a bell or buzzer sounds.

Power Levels

These vary between manufacturers, and operate on two different systems. The most general is pulsed power, the waves being pulsed into the cooker at different rates, ie short bursts with long rests for DEFROST. The other system is continuous energy being directed into the cooker cavity at a lower wattage.

Just as in a conventional cooker, different temperatures are needed to cook varying foods, eg casseroles are cooked at a lower temperature than roast joints (roasts). With the microwave it is, however, cooker power that is altered rather than temperature. Variable power, as these levels are known, is a common feature on microwave cookers. A cooker should have a minimum of two levels: DEFROST and HIGH.

TEMPERATURE PROBE

This is a metal probe which is plugged into a socket inside the cooker cavity, and will automatically gauge cooking times by means of temperature control. The probe end is inserted into the food, and the relevant temperature is set on a special control on the front of the cooker. The cooker will start when the start button is pressed, but will switch off automatically when the temperature inside the food is reached. It is used mainly for the cooking of meat joints (roasts) and re-heating of food. The probe has to be correctly placed in the food, so read the manufacturer's instructions carefully.

KEEP WARM CONTROLS

Food can be kept warm for an extended period of time in the cooker by operating it at a very low power level.

MEMORY

Microchip technology is very much a part of sophisticated microwave cookers. Memory programmes allow the cooker to be set for a period of time on a certain power level, and then change automatically to a different power level for another period of time. Some can be set to start cooking at a specific time, ie while you are out, and others can combine the use of the temperature probe.

COMBINATION MICROWAVE COOKERS

These cookers combine a browning element or forced air convection in the microwave cooker, to ensure that food can be browned. They are often known as fan-assisted or convection microwave cookers.

The forms of heating are operated either in sequence with the microwave or in a combined operation.

Check carefully on the types of cookware that can be used, as these cookers get hot when the heating elements or forced air convection are working.

MULTIPLE LEVEL COOKERS

In some microwave cookers it is possible to cook on two differ-ent power levels. The cooker has a shelf or rack which divides the cavity. Different foods can be cooked on each level as in a conventional cooker.

SENSOR COOKERS

By having sensors in the cavity, it is possible for the cooker to cook certain foods automatically. Meats, vegetables, fruit and fish can all be cooked just at the touch of a control. Pre-cooked foods can also be re-heated by this method. The cooker senses the temperature of the food and automatically switches off when the correct temperature is reached. These cookers can also operate as normal for the cooking of all other foods.

AUTO DEFROST

Some cookers have an AUTO DEFROST setting which automatically combines the defrost and standing cycles (see page 12). This is very successful with flat and uniform shaped foods. The food can then progress to a COOK or RE-HEAT programme.

PRE-PROGRAMMED COOKERS

These sophisticated cookers are pre-programmed to cook different foods to suit individual preference, eg joints (roasts) of beef, rare, medium or well done. They also indicate when food requires covering, stirring or turning over.

GAS MICROWAVE COOKERS

These are combination gas convection and microwave cookers which, like the electric versions, can be used as conventional or microwave cookers. The two energies can also operate simultaneously. These cookers are available as a counter-top model or as part of a free standing domestic cooker.

Microwave Cookers and Safety

Microwave cookers are safe, but they should not be mistreated or used for purposes other than the cooking, heating and defrosting of foods.

Microwave energy in a cooker is off a very low exposure, and should not be confused with other usage where the exposure is higher. The energy is kept within the cooker cavity by a system of door seals, and the cooker cannot operate until the door is closed. Microwave cookers have two or more different locks and safety devices, and if one should break down, the appliance will not work. When the catch is moved fractionally, the cooker ceases to function—just like switching off a light bulb.

All microwave cookers have to comply with stringent safety regulations on electrical safety and microwave leakage. Always buy one from a reputable manufacturer, look after it carefully, and service as necessary. Do not attempt to repair the cooker yourself.

Do not try to boil whole eggs, as they may explode.

Do not fry foods in deep fat.

Do not heat foods in a glass container without removing the lid or use a glass container with a narrow neck.

Do not heat foods in sealed plastic containers. Remove the seal or prick the plastic film.

Cooking Results

Microwave cooking methods are comparable to steaming, boiling, braising and simmering, ie all moist forms of cooking. Food will not naturally be browned or become crisp during cooking. However, there are always exceptions to the rules. A joint (roast) of beef weighing over 1.4kg/3 lb will become brown because of the extended time it is in the cooker. Bacon will be crisp if cooked on absorbent paper (paper towels) or a roasting rack. The fat of a bacon joint (roast) will be brown and crisp if a substance high in sugar is added. With a standard cooker it is possible to achieve the desired end result by pre-colouring foods, either by using a frying pan or an added colouring or by grilling (broiling) on removal from the cooker.

The flavour can be different from the same food cooked conventionally. Often it is more concentrated in the same way as vegetables which are cooked in very little water. Bacon, poultry and fish all have a more distinct taste. The amount of seasoning used, especially salt, needs to be less. Meat and vegetables should generally be seasoned after cooking as salt can cause dehydration during cooking.

Cakes and sponge puddings have a more open texture than normal, and tend to be dryer.

The standard microwave cooker does not, however, excel at cooking white bread, rich fruit cakes, double crust pies or choux pastry since they will not brown in the cooker; meringues also should be avoided because the dry heat required to set and dry them is not possible in a microwave cooker.

Cleaning the Cooker

If you are used to spending Sunday afternoon on your knees trying desperately to clean the oven, or even removing spilt milk which has burnt on to the hob (burners), you may be quite surprised at the minimal amount of cleaning required for a microwave cooker.

Apart from the occasional splattering of items such as baked beans and fat, food does not bake on to the sides of the cooker, and it is only necessary to wipe out the cooker cavity with a damp soapy cloth. Particular attention should be paid to the inside cooker door, by ensuring that the seals are kept clean and the cavity door surround is wiped sufficiently. If you do forget to clean the cooker, boil 600ml/1 pint/2½ US cups of water in it; the steam will loosen any dirt, and all you need do is to wipe out the cooker with a damp cloth.

If food is wrongly timed, it may dry out and leave a burnt smell in the cooker. This can be eliminated by boiling 600ml/1 pint/2½ US cups water with several slices of lemon in the cooker for 10 minutes.

If an accident occurs, eg you may over-time milk or soup, so that it boils over the cooking container, remove the cooker tray and clean it in warm soapy water in the sink; dry before replacing. When the tray forms the solid base of the cooker, just wipe this out.

As far as the outer casing of the cooker is concerned, an occasional wipe with a damp soapy cloth and a light polish with a duster will keep it in first class condition.

Remember to wipe the cooker, cooker tray, base and inside door each time you use the cooker.

Do not use an abrasive cleaner or wire (steel) wool on the cooker as this will scratch the surface.

Generally speaking, all cookware suitable for a microwave cooker will remain much cleaner than that used with traditional cooking methods. Dishes do not need soaking and can be easily cleaned in the sink or dishwasher. Some plastics may, however, be stained by tomato-based sauces and fruits such as blackberries and blackcurrants. A mild bleach solution or a proprietary (commercial) tea and coffee stain remover will remove all evidence of stains.

The Basics

Whether you love or hate cooking, the microwave will soon become a firm friend in the kitchen. Learning to adjust to the speed of the cooker takes a little time, so when trying a new recipe, watch what is happening inside the cooker. Open the cooker door—food will not be ruined because the cooker has stopped—just close the door and continue cooking. Stir, and turn and test the food for readiness often.

Do not be too ambitious too soon. Start by merely heating liquid and other foods before progressing to cooking. When following a recipe, always read it carefully, and check on how the food is prepared, the size of the dish and the cooking time, since all are important in achieving the desired result.

Many factors affect the timing of a recipe, the first and most important being the cooker power. Give a recipe to any two microwave cooker owners and there will be a difference in timings, depending upon the cooker, its age, the dish, temperature, the preparation of the food, and personal preference, so check the food often the first time you try a new recipe.

Factors influencing Time

Several factors affect the cooking times of foods prepared in the microwave cooker. Once you are familiar with them, microwave cooking will be easy.

STARTING TEMPERATURE OF THE FOOD

The colder the temperature of the food, the longer it will take to cook. If the food item is frozen, it will take a lot longer than one which is at refrigerated or room temperature so that cooking timings must be adjusted accordingly. Room temperatures tend to vary throughout the year, and the food and cookware that is used will also be at different temperatures at different times. This too will affect the microwave cooking time. When cooking frozen foods, always defrost first unless it is a vegetable item.

WEIGHT OF FOOD

Just as with conventional cookery, the more weight of food that goes into the cooker, the longer it will take. The cooking time for meat and poultry is calculated at so many minutes per 450g/1 lb (see pages 24–25).

AMOUNT OF FOOD

The more food put in the microwave cooker, the longer it will take to cook. There is only a set amount of energy coming into the microwave cavity. If more than one item is put in the cavity, then this energy has to be shared between all the items. Fifty per cent extra time should be allowed for every additional item, ie one chicken portion will take 5 minutes, two will take 7½ minutes.

FOOD COMPOSITION

Fats and sugars attract microwave energy more quickly than do liquids and other types of food. Therefore, if the food is high in fat and sugar, it will cook faster than those that are not. Where a food item, eg a fruit tart, has a high fat and sugar content, the inside will become hotter more quickly than the outside, so be careful not to overtime. All food to be cooked in a microwave cooker requires some moisture content, but foods that are very wet will take longer than those which have a low moisture content.

DENSITY OF THE FOOD

The thicker or closer together the fibres of the food, the longer it takes for the waves to penetrate the centre of the item. Light airy foods, such as cake or bread, will defrost and heat a lot more quickly than a dense meat item.

SIZE OF THE FOOD

Microwaves can only penetrate into food for a depth of about 3.75cm/1½ inches. Therefore, very large items of food have to be cooked not only by microwave but also by conduction of heat, ie by the heat passing from molecule to molecule. When preparing foods, eg vegetables to be cooked together, make sure that all are cut to the same shape and size.

SHAPE OF THE FOOD

The more even the food in shape, the more even will be the cooking result. Thinner parts of meat, fish and vegetables will cook more quickly. With large items of meat containing bone, ask the butcher to remove the bone and roll the joint (roast) for even cooking. With a whole chicken or poultry items, secure the legs and wings to the sides of the bird to help to cook evenly.

BONES IN MEAT AND POULTRY

Bones conduct heat into the meat so that meat which is near the bone will tend to cook more quickly than that which is not. If the bone cannot be removed from the joint (roast) or poultry, then shield the thinner end of the joint (roast) or poultry with a strip of foil, and remove this half-way through the cooking time. This is, incidentally, the one exception to the rule that metal should be avoided when using a microwave cooker.

Cooking Techniques

Most of the microwave cooking techniques will be familiar as they are also used when cooking conventionally.

STIRRING

All liquids or food contained within a liquid require stirring, as this helps the food to cook more evenly. Casseroles, custards, sauces, and even baked beans need to be stirred once or twice during their cooking or heating time, and again on removal from the cooker. Stir sauces and custards with a whisk rather than a fork. Stir in or out of the cooker.

PRICKING OR SCORING

Any whole food with a membrane or skin, such as eggs, kidneys, liver, tomatoes or jacket (baked) potatoes, should be pricked gently with a cocktail stick (toothpick), or scored to prevent the food from bursting.

PLACING THE FOOD

The more evenly spaced the food is in the cooker, the quicker and more evenly it will re-heat or cook. Individual items, eg fairy (cup) cakes, jacket (baked) potatoes or stuffed tomatoes should be placed in a circle, slightly separated. The ends of chops, poultry and fish should overlap or point towards the centre of the cooker, to ensure that the thin ends are cooked at the same speed as the thicker ends.

COVERING THE FOOD

Cover dishes when defrosting, heating and cooking if you want the moisture to be kept in, ie for fish, vegetables and meat. Heat and cook, uncovered, when you want the food to remain dry, ie bread, cakes and pizzas.

TURNING OF FOOD

Some large items of food cook better if they are turned over once or twice during cooking. This applies mainly to poultry and joints (roasts) of meat.

TURNING AROUND

If your cooker does not have a turntable, check with the manufacturer's instructions as to whether the food should be turned around during cooking. If cooking cakes or sponge puddings, it may be advisable in some microwave cookers to do so to achieve an even rising.

STANDING TIME

Food continues cooking, heating or defrosting on removal from the cooker. The standing time will depend on how long the food has been in the cooker. This is an important aspect of cooking in a microwave, especially with meat cookery, so always follow the instructions as the food will not be finished cooking until after the standing time is finished. Stand food, covered, generally.

RE-HEATING

Food re-heated in the cooker will taste and look as fresh as when it was first cooked. Everything from individual portions on plates for late arrivals to a baby's bottle can be heated safely in the cooker.

Defrosting

The microwave cooker is the perfect partner of the freezer. Meals can be produced for unexpected visitors, or prepared in advance, so that anyone can defrost and re-heat. No longer do you need to plan a day ahead what to take out for a meal, as even a large joint (roast) or casserole can be defrosted in an hour or so.

As the cooker defrosts both pre-cooked and raw foods, many owners take advantage of this by conventional batch-baking of chops, sausages, hamburgers and chicken portions which are then ready to defrost and re-heat for a quick meal. It is also sensible to freeze those items that the microwave does not excel at, such as pastry flan (tart) cases, or pancakes that can be used with sweet or savoury fillings. All the prepared dishes, eg soups and pastas, recommended by the manufacturers for freezing can be defrosted and heated, but care should be taken with their preparation and freezing.

Freeze food in containers suitable for the microwave cooker. If not using the cooking/serving dish, use disposable plastic freezer/microwave dishes. Most of these are re-usable several times if the manufacturer's instructions are followed. Keep the food compact in shape, eg chicken portions or meatballs should not protrude too much out of the sauce; otherwise the dish will defrost and re-heat unevenly.

All food should be pre-cooked when freezing individual portions on plates. Ensure that the food is well chilled before freezing. Cover with clingfilm (plastic wrap), or slide into a freezer bag, securing the bag with a tag, but remember to remove this before defrosting as it may be plastic-covered metal. Remember also to label the food.

Before defrosting food in the microwave cooker, loosen any coverings, and break up with a fork, soups, casseroles, sauces and solid blocks of raw meat as soon as possible to quicken the defrosting cycle. Use DEFROST, a special low power, and do not rush the process by heating on HIGH power for extended periods. If you are in a hurry for a joint (roast) or casserole, operate the cooker on HIGH power for 2–3 minutes per 450g/1 lb before turning down to DEFROST. Turn the food over, and check carefully during the cycle for any signs of cooking.

After defrosting, leave the food to stand for the recommended time (see your manufacturer's instruction book). If food starts cooking before it is completely defrosted, the end result will be uneven.

Allow the food plenty of standing time to equalize in temperature. This is especially important with poultry which should never be cooked until completely defrosted.

Food that has been frozen in a home freezer will take a lot longer to defrost than the same food item which has been frozen commercially.

What To Cook In

One of the joys of owning a microwave cooker is the variety of containers that you can use for cooking. Many suitable dishes will already be in your kitchen, dining room or cupboards. However, you cannot use metal pots and pans, including all cake tins (pans) and other pieces of baking equipment. These have the effect of blocking the microwaves and if metal is used repeatedly in the microwave cooker, it will then damage the interior.

Many materials can be used for cookware, far more than in a conventional oven. Materials such as plastic, glass and pottery allow the microwaves to pass through them to the food with varying degrees of efficiency, some being more successful than others. You can only use paper and wood for short-term re-heating of foods. Stronger materials such as glass or durable plastics must be used when cooking foods with a high fat and sugar content.

The shape of the container is important to ensure even cooking—the rounder the dishes the better, oval coming a close second. If a dish is square or oblong, food can be overcooked because the heat is trapped in the corners. The rounded bases of jugs (measuring cups), bowls and casseroles mean far less stirring of the ingredients as the food is not being overcooked. Straight-sided dishes are preferable to sloping-sided dishes as these provide a uniform depth of food.

Contrary to popular belief, dishes do get hot in the microwave by conduction of heat from the food to the dish, especially if the dish has a lid. Many foods need to be covered during heating, so look for cookware with handles or a rim as these will not get hot. A rim, feet or concave base on the bottom of the cookware also helps the microwaves to penetrate right into the centre of the food. When buying a dish to use for cooking, check the label to ensure the dish is microwave proof.

When choosing a specific dish for a recipe, make sure that it is the right size, since any thinner or liquid parts will tend to overcook before the main bulk of the food is completely ready if the food is not spread out evenly over the dish.

Ranges of cookware, specifically designed for the microwave cooker and for storage in the freezer, are available. Most can be used in a combination cooker up to certain temperatures. If in doubt, however, check the instruction book.

The most popular item is the roasting rack, which is usually made of plastic. This is used for the cooking of meat. The dish is either a solid round or square shape with ridges in the base, or has a separate rack which fits into the base of the dish. The rack allows the juices from the meat to run into the bottom of the dish, and ensures that the meat is not sitting in its own juices when cooking. This gives a more even end result to the meat. Some of these dishes are available with a dome for covering the food.

Ring-shaped dishes are available in microwave plastic and in heat-resistant glass. The centre is domed, so that when either cakes or a rice ring are turned out, there is a hole in the centre. These dishes are also useful for making jellies (gelatin dishes).

Two other helpful items for the microwave owner are the browning/searing dish and a microwave thermometer. The browning dish is available in different sizes and shapes. It is the only piece of cookware which, when heated by itself, becomes hot in the microwave cooker. Food pressed on to its surface will be sealed and coloured. The food is then turned over for the other side to colour, and at the same time cook by the microwave energy. It is only suitable for fairly flat foods such as chops, bacon or fried eggs.

The microwave thermometer is made in either a light metal or in plastic and has been designed specifically for use in the microwave cooker. It must not be used in a conventional oven, nor may a conventional thermometer be used in the microwave cooker. This is a useful addition if you intend to use the microwave cooker for meat cookery.

COVERING FOOD–SUITABLE COVERS

Many of the recipes in this book recommend covering the foods. This will help to quicken the cooking process, and equalize the temperature within the dish as well as retaining moisture.

For all recipes where a covering is necessary, use the dish lid, an upside-down plate, or clingfilm (plastic wrap) placed loosely over the dish. When cooking joints (roasts) of meat, bacon or poultry, use the domed lid which accompanies some roasting racks, or a roasting bag which has been slit along one side.

Use foil to cover joints (roasts) of meat, bacon and poultry during standing time.

Adapting Conventional Recipes for the Microwave Cooker

Adapting recipes for use in the microwave cooker takes a little bit of experimentation, but if you have a family favourite you wish to convert, then it is well worth the effort. Remember however, that results may differ from those achieved by conventional cooking, so that it is best not to experiment with your own recipes until you are familiar with all the general techniques of microwave cookery.

Unfortunately, it is not possible to give a general conversion chart to cover all types of food, but the following pointers are guidelines to success.

Select foods which you know cook well by microwave. These are foods which would normally be poached, steamed or boiled, and cooked generally in a covered dish. Do not try to convert recipes requiring a crisp finish that are either baked or roasted, as you will probably be disappointed by the end result.

Try to find a similar microwave recipe that can act as a guide to the size of dish you need and the amount of cooking time. You may find that you need to alter some of the ingredients, perhaps using less seasoning and less liquid because not so much evaporation takes place during microwave cooking. Remember that further seasoning can be added after cooking if you have not put enough in at the beginning. You may also find that some ingredients need to be pre-cooked first, eg rice, as this will take longer to cook than the vegetables that you may be using in the same recipe.

Start checking to see if the dish is cooked, one quarter of the time that it normally takes in the conventional cooker. Cakes and suet items should be checked after 4 minutes. Remember that food will continue to cook after it is taken out of the microwave cooker. Less fat can also be used in a recipe generally. This is especially important when sautéing meat and vegetables for a casserole. The amount of fat can be cut by half.

Cookware Chart
Durable Cookware

Material	Suitable Foods	Safe in Freezer	Suitable for Defrosting	Suitable for Heating	Suitable for Cooking	Comments
Wood/straw	Bread/biscuits Kebabs	No	No	Yes	No	Use wooden or bamboo skewers for kebabs instead of metal
Melamine	Not suitable	No	No	No	No	—
Heat-resistant glass	All foods	,,	Yes	,,	Yes	Suitable also for combination cookers
Glass/ceramic	All foods	Yes	,,	,,	,,	Suitable also for combination cookers
Pottery/porcelain/ stoneware	All foods	No	,,	,,	,,	Avoid unglazed items or those with a metallic sheen. These will get very hot during longer cooking periods
Plastic sold especially for the microwave cooker	All foods, but can be affected by high fats and sugar temperatures	Yes	,,	,,	,,	All can be used in combination cookers but only up to certain temperatures

Notes
1) Where stated above that a material is suitable for a combination cooker, check the recommended cookware temperature before using.
2) If you are not sure of the suitability of a piece of cookware, use this test. Put the cookware into the cooker. Pour 300ml/½ pint/1¼ US cups water into a heat-resistant jug (cup). Put the jug (cup) in or next to the cookware. Heat for 1 minute. If the water becomes hot and the dish remains cool, it is microwave safe. If the dish is hot, do not use it.

Cookware Chart
Disposable Materials

Material	Suitable Foods	Safe in Freezer	Suitable for Defrosting	Suitable for Heating	Suitable for Cooking	Comments
Paper kitchen towels	Bread-based products, jacket (baked) potatoes and bacon	No	Yes	Yes	Yes	—
Paper plates and cups	Liquids and bread-based products	Yes	,,	,,	,,	Use for short time only
Plastic foam trays	Foods without fat or sugar	Yes	,,	,,	see Comments	Limited cooking use as very hot food will buckle
Clingfilm (plastic wrap)	All foods	see Comments	,,	,,	Yes	Use only for covering dishes. Freezer film is better for freezer
Freezer bags/film (wrap)	All foods	Yes	,,	No	No	Always loosen from around food during defrosting
Roasting bags/film (wrap)	All meats	Not applicable	No	Yes	Yes	For covering joints (roasts) and poultry during cooking; stops splashing and helps colouring. Can be used in combination cooker when heating element or warm air is operating
Greaseproof (waxed) paper/layering tissue	Cakes and pastry	Yes	,,	No	,,	Use for lining cake, flan (tart) and loaf dishes
Boilable bags	All foods	,,	Yes	Yes	,,	Always prick the bag before putting in cooker
Ovenable board	All foods	,,	,,	,,	,,	Some can also be used in combination cooker up to certain temperatures
Plastic dishes sold especially for the microwave cooker and freezer	All foods, but can be affected by high fats and sugar temperatures	,,	,,	,,	,,	Do not cover tightly during heating. Dishes sometimes prone to staining. Some can be used in combination cooker up to certain temperatures

HELPFUL HINTS

Ask any microwave owner what they like most about their cooker and they will forget to mention the splendid vegetables that come out of it, but enthuse over the way it will dry herbs in minutes, or they will forget how quickly it cooks a joint (roast) of beef and only remember how it re-heats a cup of coffee.

To dry herbs, spread out on absorbent paper (paper towels), cover with another sheet, and put in the microwave for 2–3 minutes on HIGH. Remember that drying will continue after removal from the cooker. If more drying is required, give a further 1–2 minutes on HIGH.

Use an electric kettle whenever a quantity of boiling water is needed–for example, in cooking rice, pasta or soups.

Prepare the fillings and toppings for toasted sandwiches, hamburgers and hotdogs in the cooker, but use an electric toaster or grill (broiler) for the bases.

A pre-heated grill (broiler) is invaluable for giving many fish, pasta, cheese and pudding recipes additional colour and crispness, but do not use this for cakes as the heat would only dry out the surface.

Use a frying pan to pre-brown and seal vegetables, meats for casseroles or when serving without a sauce or without garnish. Otherwise the result can look a little pale and uninteresting.

Par-cook potatoes by microwave before roasting, and use a conventional oven to accentuate the colouring of a Sunday roast and make it crisp during its standing time.

Par-cook chips (French fries), vegetables, chicken and meat portions in the microwave, drain and coat as required. Continue by frying at a high setting for a short time to complete the cooking and add a crisp finish. Less oil is absorbed into the food, and you can also be sure that the centre of the item is cooked.

FURTHER USES OF THE MICROWAVE COOKER

Warming flour for making bread
Warming jam
Warming sugar for making jam
Softening butter for spreading on to bread
Softening margarine, cream cheese or butter for use in cooking (check carefully after a few seconds and give longer as required)
Heating the marmalade jar to remove that last spoonful
Heating honey, liquid glucose and golden syrup for easy measuring
Dissolving gelatine (see French Cream Rice on page 63)
Melting chocolate and marshmallows
Softening hard brown sugar or dates
Warming marzipan before rolling it out to decorate a cake
Blanching small quantities of vegetables before freezing
Warming citrus fruits to give more juice before squeezing
Opening mussels
Drying breadcrumbs
Warming a baby's bottle containing milk or fruit juice (remember to test the temperature before feeding)
Heating baby food in glass containers (only 35–40 seconds on HIGH, but test the temperature before serving).

Beginning A Meal

Many people tend to choose a cold first course, particularly when entertaining, so that more time can be spent with guests, or in preparing a hot main course dish. With a microwave cooker, this is no longer necessary as soups and other first courses can be made well in advance and re-heated quickly when required. It also makes it easier to give those final touches.

Stock for soups can be made by cooking bones, seasoning and water for 40 minutes on HIGH, followed by about 40 minutes standing time.

When making soups in the cooker, choose a large container as liquids tend to rise when boiling. Soups can be cooked in the serving tureen or container, thereby reducing the amount of washing up.

Swiss Eggs

Metric/imperial		American
1×5ml spoon/ 1 teaspoon	anchovy essence (paste)	1 teaspoon
4× size 2	eggs	4 large
50g/2 oz	hard cheese, grated	$\frac{1}{2}$ cup

Put $\frac{1}{2}$×2.5ml spoon/$\frac{1}{4}$ teaspoon anchovy essence (paste) into each of four small ramekin dishes. Break an egg into each dish, and pierce the yolk. Cover with the grated cheese. Cook for 1$\frac{1}{4}$–2 minutes on HIGH and stand for 1 minute or so before serving.

Serve with fingers (strips) of buttered toast.

Scrambled Eggs with Smoked Salmon

Metric/imperial		American
	8×1.25cm/$\frac{1}{2}$ inch thick slices white bread	
100g/4 oz	butter	1 stick
5× size 2	eggs, beaten	5 large
	salt, freshly ground pepper	
2×15ml spoons/ 2 tablespoons	single (light) cream	2 tablespoons
100g/4 oz	smoked salmon, shredded	$\frac{1}{4}$ lb
	4 stoned (pitted) black olives, halved	
	chopped parsley	

Cut out eight rounds from the bread slices with a plain or fluted 7.5cm/3 inch pastry cutter. Melt 50g/2 oz/$\frac{1}{2}$ US stick of the butter in a frying pan, and fry the bread rounds until golden-brown. Put on absorbent paper (paper towels).

Put the remaining butter with the beaten eggs, salt, pepper and cream in a jug (measuring cup). Add the salmon, and beat with a fork. Cook for 4 minutes on MEDIUM. Stir, and return to the cooker for another 4–5 minutes or until the eggs are thick and creamy. Stir on removal from the cooker.

Heat the fried bread on a roasting rack or absorbent paper (paper towels) for 1 minute on HIGH. Put the scrambled eggs on the bread rounds, arrange the olives on top, and sprinkle with the parsley.

Walnut Stuffed Mushrooms

Metric/imperial		American
75g/3 oz	softened butter	6 tablespoons
	12×5cm/2 inch button mushrooms, stalks removed and chopped	
50g/2 oz	freshly made breadcrumbs	1 cup
75g/3 oz	walnuts, chopped	¾ cup
	2 stalks celery, chopped finely	
2×5ml spoons/ 2 teaspoons	chopped chives	2 teaspoons
1×5ml spoon/ 1 teaspoon	lemon juice	1 teaspoon
50g/2 oz	hard cheese, grated	½ cup
	salt, freshly ground black pepper	

Melt 50g/2 oz/½ US stick of the butter in a large shallow dish for 1 minute on HIGH. Mix the mushroom stalks with the breadcrumbs, walnuts, celery, chives, lemon juice and cheese. Season to taste. Mix in the remaining butter. Fill the mushrooms with the mixture, and arrange in the dish, coating them with the butter in the base. Heat for 6–8 minutes on MEDIUM. Serve hot.

Baby Onions in Wine

Metric/imperial		American
450g/1 lb	shallots, peeled	1 lb
4×15ml spoons/ 4 tablespoons	white wine	¼ cup
4×15ml spoons/ 4 tablespoons	chicken stock	¼ cup
	a few drops lemon juice	
2×15ml spoons/ 2 tablespoons	concentrated tomato purée (paste)	2 tablespoons
2×15ml spoons/ 2 tablespoons	cooking oil	2 tablespoons
	a good pinch of sugar	
	salt, freshly ground pepper	
	GARNISH chopped parsley	

Put all the ingredients in a medium casserole. Cook, covered, for 8 minutes on HIGH, and then, uncovered, on HIGH for a further 7 minutes or until the onions are soft. Stir once during the cycle and on removal from the cooker. Serve hot or cold, garnished with chopped parsley.

Note This recipe can also be used as a vegetable accompaniment.

Bacon Wrapped Corn-on-the-Cob

Serves 2

Metric/imperial		American
	2 cobs of corn	
2×15ml spoons/ 2 tablespoons	water	2 tablespoons
25g/1 oz	melted butter	2 tablespoons
	salt, freshly ground black pepper	
	2 rashers (slices) back (Canadian) bacon, rinds removed	

Put the cobs in a dish with the water, and cook, covered, for 6 minutes on HIGH. Remove from the cooker, brush with the butter, and season with salt and pepper. Wrap one bacon rasher (slice) round each cob. Put the joined side of bacon down on to a roasting rack, and cook, uncovered, for a further 6 minutes on HIGH. Serve immediately, with additional butter.

Note For four servings, double the ingredients and increase the time by about fifty per cent.

Corn and Pepper Soup

Serves 2

Metric/imperial		American
25g/1 oz	butter	2 tablespoons
	1 stalk of celery, chopped	
	1 small onion, chopped	
	½ red pepper, de-seeded and chopped	
2×15ml spoons/ 2 tablespoons	plain (all-purpose) flour	2 tablespoons
1×5ml spoon/ 1 teaspoon	lemon juice	1 teaspoon
300ml/½ pint	vegetable stock	1¼ cups
150ml/¼ pint	milk	⅔ cup
200g/7 oz	canned whole kernel sweetcorn, drained	scant 1½ cups
	salt, freshly ground white pepper	

Melt the butter in a medium casserole for 1 minute on HIGH. Add the celery, onion and red pepper, and cook, covered, for 5 minutes on MEDIUM. Blend in the flour. Stir in the lemon juice, stock and milk, and cook for 7 minutes on HIGH, stirring after 3 minutes and at the end of the cycle. Add the sweetcorn and seasoning, and heat for a further 4–5 minutes on HIGH before serving.

Bacon wrapped Corn-on-the-Cob

CREAM OF TURKEY SOUP

Metric/imperial		American
1×15ml spoon/ 1 tablespoon	cooking oil	1 tablespoon
	2 rashers (slices) streaky bacon, rinds removed and chopped	
	1 small onion, chopped finely	
	2 stalks celery, chopped finely	
600ml/1 pint	turkey stock (see **Note**)	2½ cups
225g/8 oz	turkey meat, cooked and cut into small pieces	½ lb
300ml/½ pint	milk	1¼ cups
	salt, freshly ground pepper	
	chopped parsley	

Put the oil, bacon, onion and celery in a large round dish. Cook, covered, for 6 minutes on MEDIUM. Stir in the stock and turkey. Cook, covered, for 8 minutes on HIGH, then on MEDIUM for 20 minutes, and stir half-way through the cooking cycle. Purée the soup in a blender or pass through a sieve until smooth. Stir in the milk, return to the cooker, and heat on HIGH for 10 minutes. Season to taste. Garnish with the parsley.

Note This is a delicious soup at any time but especially useful after Christmas.

Prepare the turkey stock using the bones of the turkey.

CHILLED WATERCRESS SOUP

Metric/imperial		American
25g/1 oz	butter	2 tablespoons
	1 medium onion, chopped finely	
225g/8 oz	potato, peeled and diced	½ lb
	2 bunches watercress, washed and any coarse stalks removed, and leaves chopped	
450ml/¾ pint	chicken stock	2 cups
300ml/½ pint	milk	1¼ cups
	salt, freshly ground pepper	
150ml/¼ pint	single (light) cream	⅔ cup

Put the butter and onion into a medium casserole, and cook, covered, for 5 minutes on MEDIUM. Add the potato, and cook for a further 3 minutes on MEDIUM. Add the watercress to the potato mixture, cover and cook for a further 5 minutes on HIGH. Stir in the stock, milk and seasoning. Cook, covered, for 20 minutes on HIGH. Stir every 10 minutes. Purée the soup in a blender or pass through a sieve until smooth. Stir in most of the cream. Chill in a refrigerator. Stir before serving, swirled with the remaining cream.

MEAT AND POULTRY CENTRE PIECES

Cooking meat in the microwave cooker is a great time saver. Less shrinkage and weight loss occurs, especially in poultry which does not have a shrivelled appearance at the end of cooking. Joints (roasts) and whole poultry come out of the cooker with succulent meat and a very fresh taste.

Because the cooking time is so quick in a microwave cooker, meat does not become as brown as it would do in a conventional oven. Help has, therefore, to be given by using either the special proprietary (commercial) brands of seasonings and colourings or inventing your own, such as honey, sherry, soy sauce, Worcestershire sauce or mustard, to brush or sprinkle over the meat before putting it into the cooker. Joints (roasts) of beef weighing 1.4kg/3 lb or more tend to colour naturally in the microwave because the cooking time is proportionately longer. On removal from a microwave cooker, joints (roasts) can, of course, be placed under a grill (broiler) or in a hot oven to brown and crisp the skin.

Single items of meat should be pre-browned in a frying pan or under a grill (broiler), or they can be cooked on a microwave browning dish which will brown and cook the food at the same time. This is really only suitable for flat items.

When adding seasoning to meat, it is best not to add salt until cooking is complete as this can dehydrate the surface of the meat.

When choosing meat, look for joints (roasts) which are round and even in shape. The more even a joint (roast), the easier it is to cook in a microwave cooker. Anything which contains a bone, especially something like a leg of lamb, should be boned and rolled, or a strip of foil can be placed along the thinner end; this is removed half-way through the cooking time.

Do ensure that all meat is completely defrosted before cooking in a microwave cooker. This is especially important with chicken and other poultry items.

It is best not to stuff a bird before putting it into the cooker. This is because the cavity within the bird adds to the depth in which the microwaves have to penetrate, and will, therefore, affect the cooking time. Cook the stuffing separately during the bird's standing time. This ensures that the microwaves get right through to the centre. It is also inadvisable to cook a turkey or goose larger than 5.4–6.8kg/12–15 lb, as this is the maximum weight that can be cooked successfully in a microwave cooker.

Meat Cooking Chart

Unless the cooker has a temperature probe, a microwave meat thermometer is recommended for accurate meat cookery. This should be inserted into the centre of the meat parallel to any bone structure. Remove the meat from the cooker when the recommended temperature is reached. If not using a thermometer, follow the recommended cooking times. More time can be given if necessary after the standing time.

Meat unboned unrolled	Degree of cooking	Cooking time per 450g/1 lb	Temperature on removal from cooker	Special points
Beef	Rare	2 minutes HIGH/7–8 minutes MEDIUM	55°C/130°F	Stand covered in foil for 15–20 minutes before serving
	Medium	2 minutes HIGH/9–10 minutes MEDIUM	65°C/150°F	,,
	Well done	2 minutes HIGH/12–13 minutes MEDIUM	70°C/160°F	,,
Lamb/veal		2 minutes HIGH/10–12 minutes MEDIUM	75°C/170°F	,,
Pork		2 minutes HIGH/11–13 minutes MEDIUM	65°C/150°F	,,
Gammon/ bacon (ham)		2 minutes HIGH/9–10 minutes MEDIUM	60°C/145°F	,,

Note Boned and rolled joints (roasts) will generally take 1–2 minutes longer per 450g/1 lb than the above timings.

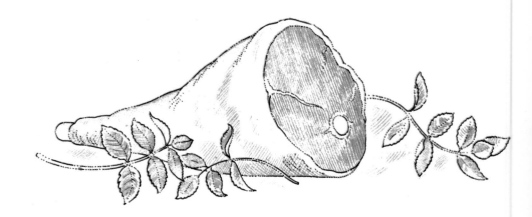

Poultry and Game Cooking Chart

All poultry and game should be put on a microwave roasting rack, or on an upside-down plate. This helps to eliminate uneven cooking. Cover with a slit roasting bag or microwave dome to promote natural colouring and set any added colouring.

To prevent overcooking of wings and thin ends of portions, wrap in foil strips, which should be removed half-way through the cooking time. Secure the legs and wings to the side of the bird so that it cooks evenly.

Poultry and Game	Cooking time per 450g/1 lb	Special points
Chicken (whole)	6–8 minutes HIGH	Cover in foil after cooking, then stand for 15–20 minutes
Chicken (portions)	6–7 minutes HIGH	Arrange on a roasting rack, thicker parts towards the outer edge. Cover in foil after cooking, then stand for 5–10 minutes
Duck (whole)	7–9 minutes HIGH	Start cooking breast side down, and turn over half-way through cooking time. Cover in foil after cooking, then stand for 15–20 minutes
Capon	6–8 minutes HIGH	,,
Turkey/goose (maximum size 6.8kg/15 lb)	7–9 minutes HIGH	,,
Game, ie pheasant, quail and grouse	6–8 minutes HIGH	Cover in foil after cooking, then stand for 15–20 minutes

Note Venison, hare and rabbit are unsuitable for roasting in a microwave cooker.

Beef Bourguignonne

Metric/imperial		American
3×15ml spoons/ 3 tablespoons	cooking oil	3 tablespoons
1.25kg/2½ lb	rolled topside (top round) **or** sirloin of beef	2½ lb
	8 baby onions	
175g/6 oz	streaky bacon, rinds removed and chopped	¾ cup
2×15ml spoons/ 2 tablespoons	plain (all-purpose) flour	2 tablespoons
300ml/½ pint	dry red wine	1¼ cups
300ml/½ pint	stock	1¼ cups
	bouquet garni	
	salt, freshly ground pepper	
225g/8 oz	button mushrooms	2 cups
	GARNISH chopped parsley	

Heat the oil in a large frying pan, and pre-brown the beef by rolling it over several times to sear the outside. Put the beef into a large casserole, and add the onions and bacon.

Stir the flour into the oil in the frying pan, and cook for 1 minute. Add the wine and stock, and bring to the boil. Add the bouquet garni, salt and pepper. Pour the liquid over the beef. Cover, and cook for 15 minutes on HIGH. Turn the cooker down to MEDIUM, and cook for a further hour. Turn the meat over in the casserole every 30 minutes. Add the mushrooms to the casserole during the last 30 minutes of cooking. Stand for 15 minutes before carving. Serve garnished with parsley.

Beef Olives

Metric/imperial		American
	salt, freshly ground black pepper	
	8 thin slices topside (top round) of beef	
2×15ml spoons/ 2 tablespoons	cooking oil	2 tablespoons
	2 medium onions, sliced	
25g/1 oz	flour	¼ cup
900ml/1½ pints	beef stock	3¾ cups
	chopped parsley	
50g/2 oz	STUFFING freshly made breadcrumbs	1 cup
	milk	
75g/3 oz	ham, chopped	generous ½ cup
2×5ml spoons/ 2 teaspoons	capers, chopped	2 teaspoons
	grated rind of 1 lemon	
	2 hard-boiled eggs, chopped	

To make the stuffing, soak the crumbs for 10 minutes in the milk, then squeeze out. Mix with the remaining ingredients.

Season the slices of beef, and spread with the stuffing. Roll up, and tie each beef olive with string.

Heat the oil in a frying pan, and brown the meat on all sides, then put into a medium casserole with the onions. Sprinkle the flour into the remaining oil, and cook for a few minutes until brown. Stir in the stock gradually, and bring to the boil. Pour over the meat and onions. Cook, covered, for 15 minutes on HIGH, then for 2 hours on DEFROST, stirring every 45 minutes. Remove from the stock, and discard the strings. Return it to the casserole, and leave to stand for 10 minutes. Garnish with parsley.

FRUITY LAMB CASSEROLE

Serves 2

Metric/imperial		American
	4 small lamb chops	
1×15ml spoon/ 1 tablespoon	cooking oil	1 tablespoon
	1 small onion, chopped	
	1 stalk of celery, chopped	
1×15ml spoon/ 1 tablespoon	golden (corn) syrup	1 tablespoon
1×5ml spoon/ 1 teaspoon	prepared English mustard	1 teaspoon
	1 small cooking apple, peeled, cored and diced	
25g/1 oz	raisins	1½ tablespoons
2×5ml spoons/ 2 teaspoons	cornflour (cornstarch)	2 teaspoons
	strained juice and grated rind of 1 orange	
150ml/¼ pint	chicken stock	⅔ cup
	salt, freshly ground pepper	
	orange slices	

Brown the chops on both sides in a hot frying pan.

Heat the oil with the onion and celery for 5 minutes in a shallow dish on MEDIUM. Add the syrup, mustard, apple and raisins. Mix the cornflour (cornstarch) to a smooth paste with the orange juice and stock. Stir into the onion mixture. Heat for 6 minutes on HIGH, stirring half-way through the cycle and on removal.

Add the lamb chops, orange rind and seasoning, and cook, covered, on MEDIUM for 20–25 minutes or until the chops are tender. Garnish with orange slices.

LIVER IN CREAM SAUCE

Serves 2

Metric/imperial		American
225–275g/ 8–10 oz	lambs' liver, pricked **or** scored	½–¾ lb
2×15ml spoons/ 2 tablespoons	seasoned flour	2 tablespoons
1×15ml spoon/ 1 tablespoon	cooking oil	1 tablespoon
15g/½ oz	butter	1 tablespoon
	1 medium onion, sliced	
150ml/¼ pint	stock	⅔ cup
2×15ml spoons/ 2 tablespoons	vermouth	2 tablespoons
50g/2 oz	bacon, rinds removed and chopped	¼ cup
50g/2 oz	button mushrooms	½ cup
4×15ml spoons/ 4 tablespoons	single (light) cream	¼ cup
	GARNISH chopped chives	

Coat the liver with the seasoned flour. Melt the oil and butter together in a frying pan, and fry the onion gently until golden-brown. Brown the outer surfaces of the liver in the pan, then put the liver and the onion into a shallow casserole. Stir the stock into the pan gradually, and bring to the boil. Stir in the vermouth, and pour over the liver. Add the bacon and mushrooms to the casserole. Cook, covered on HIGH for 3 minutes, and then on MEDIUM for 7–10 minutes or until the liver is tender. Remove from the cooker, stir in the cream, and serve sprinkled with the chives.

Note Liver is especially good when cooked in a microwave cooker as it does not toughen. The vermouth adds a special flavour to this dish.

LAMB KEBABS

Metric/imperial		American
450g/1 lb	lean fillet **or** shoulder of lamb, cubed	1 lb
	16 button (small white) onions	
150ml/¼ pint	red wine vinegar	⅔ cup
3 × 15ml spoons/ 3 tablespoons	water	3 tablespoons
2 × 15ml spoons/ 2 tablespoons	apricot jam	2 tablespoons
2 × 15ml spoons/ 2 tablespoons	chutney	2 tablespoons
2 × 15ml spoons/ 2 tablespoons	soft brown sugar	2 tablespoons
1 × 15ml spoon/ 1 tablespoon	curry powder	1 tablespoon
	8 small orange slices, unpeeled	
	4 small lemon slices, unpeeled	
	8 button mushrooms	
	vegetable oil	

Put the lamb and onions into a bowl, and leave on one side.

Mix together the vinegar, water, apricot jam, chutney, sugar and curry powder in a medium bowl, and heat for 5 minutes on HIGH. Remove from the cooker, and stir well, then add the lamb mixture. Leave to stand for 2 hours.

Drain the lamb and onions, and thread on to four wooden skewers with the sliced fruit and mushrooms. Brush with oil and a little of the marinade. Put the kebabs on the roasting rack, and cook for 8–10 minutes on HIGH. Brush with the marinade halfway through the cooking time.

Heat the marinade in a small bowl for 2–3 minutes on HIGH. Serve immediately with the kebabs.

KIDNEYS WITH SAUSAGES

Metric/imperial		American
2 × 15ml spoons/ 2 tablespoons	cooking oil	2 tablespoons
	8 lambs' kidneys, skinned and halved (see **Note**)	
	4 chipolata sausages, each twisted centrally and halved	
	8 button (small white) onions, peeled	
1 × 15ml spoon/ 1 tablespoon	plain (all-purpose) flour	1 tablespoon
300ml/½ pint	beef stock	1¼ cups
2 × 15ml spoons/ 2 tablespoons	dry sherry	2 tablespoons
1 × 15ml spoon/ 1 tablespoon	concentrated tomato purée (paste)	1 tablespoon
	salt, freshly ground pepper	

Heat the oil in a frying pan, and gently fry the kidneys, sausages and onions until brown. Put into a medium casserole.

Stir the flour into the hot juices remaining in the frying pan, and cook gently. Add the stock gradually, stirring until smooth. Bring to the boil, and stir in the sherry and tomato purée (paste). Season to taste.

Pour the stock over the kidneys, cover with a lid, and cook for 12 minutes on HIGH. Leave to stand for 5 minutes before serving.

Note Snip out the white core of the kidneys with scissors.

Lamb Kebabs

Veal with Tarragon Sauce

Metric/imperial		American
65g/2½ oz	butter	5 tablespoons
40g/1½ oz	flour	6 tablespoons
300ml/½ pint	chicken stock	1¼ cups
2 × 15ml spoons/ 2 tablespoons	tarragon vinegar	2 tablespoons
1 × 5ml spoon/ 1 teaspoon	fresh tarragon, chopped	1 teaspoon
25g/1 oz	Parmesan cheese, finely grated	¼ cup
	salt, freshly ground pepper	
	4 veal escalopes (scallops) (100g/4 oz each approx)	
	seasoned flour	
150ml/¼ pint	single (light) cream	⅔ cup

Melt 40g/1½ oz/3 US tablespoons of the butter in a medium casserole for 1 minute on HIGH. Stir in the flour. Stir in the stock and vinegar gradually. Cook on HIGH for 5–6 minutes or until the sauce boils, stirring well every 2 minutes. Stir in the tarragon, cheese, salt and pepper. Heat for a further 3 minutes on HIGH.

Coat the veal in the seasoned flour. Melt the remaining butter in the frying pan, and colour the veal quickly. Remove from the frying pan, and place in a shallow casserole.

Pour the sauce over the veal. Cook, covered, for 8 minutes on HIGH. Stir in the cream, and cook, uncovered, for a further 9 minutes on MEDIUM. Stir gently before serving.

Loin Pork Chops with Red Cabbage

Metric/imperial		American
550g/1¼ lb	red cabbage, chopped finely	1¼ lb
	1 onion, chopped finely	
1 × 15ml spoon/ 1 tablespoon	cooking oil	1 tablespoon
	1 cooking apple, peeled, cored and sliced	
150ml/¼ pint	red wine	⅔ cup
	salt, freshly ground pepper	
	4 loin pork chops (175g/6 oz each, approx)	
3 × 15ml spoons/ 3 tablespoons	honey	3 tablespoons

Put the cabbage, onion and oil into a shallow casserole. Cook, covered, for 5 minutes on HIGH. Add the apple, wine and seasoning, then cook for a further 10 minutes on HIGH. Add the pork chops, and coat with the honey. Cook, covered, on MEDIUM for 30–40 minutes or until the chops are tender.

Gammon (Ham) Steaks with Apple

Metric/imperial		American
	2 cooking apples, peeled, cored and sliced	
	1 onion, sliced	
150ml/¼ pint	cider	⅔ cup
4×150g/5 oz	smoked gammon (ham) steaks, rinds removed	4×5 oz
50g/2 oz	Demerara (light brown) sugar	¼ cup
1×5ml spoon/ 1 teaspoon	prepared English mustard	1 teaspoon

Put the apples and onion into a large shallow casserole, and add the cider. Snip the fat of the gammon (ham) steaks at intervals to prevent curling, and lay on top of the apple mixture. Cook for 10 minutes on HIGH.

Mix together the sugar and the mustard, and add 2×15ml spoons/2 tablespoons of the liquid from the casserole. Cook on HIGH for a further 8–10 minutes or until the gammon (ham) is completely cooked.

Apricot Hock

Metric/imperial		American
	half hock of bacon (ham), unsmoked (2.3kg/5 lb approx), soaked overnight and drained	
2×15ml spoons/ 2 tablespoons	apricot jam, sieved	2 tablespoons
	GARNISH halved glacé (candied) cherries	
	apricot halves	

Put the bacon (ham) hock into a shallow casserole, and cover with a microwave dome. Cook for 25 minutes on HIGH, turning over every 10 minutes. Remove from the cooker.

Drain the juices from the dish. Cut the skin off the bacon (ham). Cut a criss-cross pattern into the fat, and spread with the apricot jam. Place a strip of foil across the top of each end to prevent the edges on the top surface overcooking. Return to the cooker, uncovered, and cook for a further 20 minutes on HIGH.

On removal from the cooker, wrap in foil, and allow to stand for 20 minutes. Garnish with the glacé (candied) cherries and apricot halves.

CANTONESE SPARE RIBS

Serves 2

Metric/imperial		American
450g/1 lb	pork spare ribs, Chinese-cut	1 lb
1×15ml spoon/ 1 tablespoon	cooking oil	1 tablespoon
2×5ml spoons/ 2 teaspoons	cornflour (cornstarch)	2 teaspoons
2×15ml spoons/ 2 tablespoons	MARINADE light soy sauce	2 tablespoons
1×15ml spoon/ 1 tablespoon	tomato ketchup	1 tablespoon
1×15ml spoon/ 1 tablespoon	dry sherry	1 tablespoon
2×15ml spoons/ 2 tablespoons	strained lemon juice	2 tablespoons
1×15ml spoon/ 1 tablespoon	soft brown sugar	1 tablespoon
$\frac{1}{2}$×2.5ml spoon/ $\frac{1}{4}$ teaspoon	ground ginger	$\frac{1}{4}$ teaspoon
$1\frac{1}{2}$×15ml spoons/ $1\frac{1}{2}$ tablespoons	thin-cut marmalade	$1\frac{1}{2}$ tablespoons

To make the marinade, mix together all the ingredients in a shallow casserole.

Put the spare ribs in the marinade, and leave for 3 hours, turning several times.

Pre-heat a browning dish on HIGH for 6 minutes. Add the ribs and oil, and cook for 2 minutes on HIGH. Turn the ribs over, and cook for 8–10 minutes on HIGH. Remove the ribs from the dish.

Mix the cornflour (cornstarch) with a little of the marinade until smooth, and add to the casserole with the remaining marinade. Heat for 5 minutes on HIGH, stirring once or twice. Add the ribs, and cook, covered, on HIGH for 8 minutes or until well heated through.

32

CHICKEN WITH PEPPERS

Metric/imperial		American
1×15ml spoon/ 1 tablespoon	cooking oil	1 tablespoon
	1 green pepper, de-seeded and chopped	
	1 large onion, chopped	
550g/1¼ lb	chicken, cut into small pieces	1¼ lb
450g/1 lb	tomatoes, skinned and sliced	1 lb
1×5ml spoon/ 1 teaspoon	oregano	1 teaspoon
6×15ml spoons/ 6 tablespoons	dry white wine	6 tablespoons
1×15ml spoon/ 1 tablespoon	concentrated tomato purée (paste)	1 tablespoon
	salt, freshly ground pepper	

Put the oil, pepper and onion into a medium casserole. Cook, covered, for 10 minutes on MEDIUM. Add the remaining ingredients, and stir well. Cook, covered, for a further 20 minutes on HIGH.

Cantonese Spare Ribs **and** Chinese Medley (page 47)

Tandoori Turkey

Metric/imperial		American
	4 turkey drumsticks, skinned	
	paprika	
	MARINADE	
300ml/½ pint	yoghurt	1¼ cups
1×5ml spoon/ 1 teaspoon	garam masala	1 teaspoon
1×5ml spoon/ 1 teaspoon	salt	1 teaspoon
1×5ml spoon/ 1 teaspoon	turmeric	1 teaspoon
1×5ml spoon/ 1 teaspoon	chilli powder	1 teaspoon
	1 clove of garlic, crushed	
1×2.5ml spoon/ ½ teaspoon	ground ginger	½ teaspoon
1×15ml spoon/ 1 tablespoon	concentrated tomato purée (paste)	1 tablespoon
2×15ml spoons/ 2 tablespoons	strained lemon juice	2 tablespoons
2×15ml spoons/ 2 tablespoons	cooking oil	2 tablespoons
	GARNISH 2 lemons, cut in quarters	
	sprigs parsley	

Pat the turkey drumsticks dry with absorbent kitchen paper (paper towels), and cut deep slits in the flesh.

To make the marinade, mix together all the ingredients. Marinate the turkey drumsticks in this mixture for at least 4 hours, or overnight, in a refrigerator.

Drain the turkey drumsticks from the marinade, and place on a roasting rack. Sprinkle liberally with paprika, cover with a slit roasting bag, and cook on HIGH for 12–15 minutes or until the turkey drumsticks are cooked. Leave to stand, covered, for 10 minutes before serving. Garnish with the lemon quarters and parsley sprigs.

Duck with Honey and Chestnuts

Metric/imperial		American
	1 duck (2kg/4½ lb approx)	
150ml/¼ pint	stock	⅔ cup
150ml/¼ pint	dry white wine	⅔ cup
4×15ml spoons/ 4 tablespoons	honey	¼ cup
2×5ml spoons/ 2 teaspoons	cornflour (cornstarch)	2 teaspoons
	salt, freshly ground pepper	
	16 chestnuts, cooked (see **Note**)	

Brown the duck on all sides in a hot, dry frying pan over low heat. Place the duck on the roasting rack, cover with a slit roasting bag, and cook, breast side down, for 20 minutes on HIGH. Turn breast side up, and cook for a further 20 minutes. Leave to stand, wrapped in foil, for a further 20 minutes.

Carve the duck into four portions, and leave on one side. Remove as much fat as possible from the duck juices. Stir the stock, wine and honey into the duck juices. Mix the cornflour (cornstarch) to a smooth paste with a little water, add this to the liquid, and stir well. Heat for 5 minutes on HIGH, stirring once or twice. Season to taste. Put the duck and the cooked chestnuts in this mixture, and heat for 15 minutes on HIGH.

Note To cook the chestnuts, make a slit in the shell of each. Put eight at a time into a small bowl, cover with water, and heat on HIGH for 4–5 minutes or until the water boils, then boil for 1 minute. Stand for 10 minutes. Drain, and peel.

FISHERMAN'S CATCH

Fish and shellfish prepared in a microwave cooker are full of flavour, flaking beautifully but not falling apart. Additionally, there is no dryness and the flesh is easy to lift off the bone.

Many people associate a lingering unpleasant smell with fish cookery. By cooking fish in a microwave cooker, this will not happen.

All fish, whether in pieces or whole, is suitable for microwave cooking. When buying fish, look for even-shaped pieces and even-sized whole fish as these make for more even cooking.

Because fish cooks so quickly in a microwave cooker, it is usually cooked last when cooking a complete meal. If preparing a sauce to go with the fish, make the sauce first, leaving it to stand to be poured over the cooked fish. If you intend to re-heat the fish later, undercook it slightly to make sure it is not overcooked by re-heating.

Frozen defrosted shellfish has been used mostly in the recipes in this chapter, as it is more widely available, but fresh shellfish can, of course, be substituted.

Fish and Shellfish Cooking Chart

If cooking fish or shellfish without any liquid or sauce, always brush the skin or surface flesh with melted butter to prevent it toughening. Cook loosely covered with clingfilm (plastic wrap).

Fish or Shellfish	Cooking time on HIGH per 450g/1 lb	Special points
Whole fish	7–9 minutes	Cut the skin in several places to prevent bursting. Shield the head and tail with foil, and remove this half-way through cooking time
Fillets of fish	6–7 minutes	Overlap the thinner ends towards the centre of the dish, or put the thin parts next to or under the thick parts
Fish steaks	5–6 minutes	Overlap the thinner ends towards the centre of the dish, or put the thin parts next to or under the thick parts
Scallops	5–7 minutes	Cover with damp absorbent paper (paper towels)
Prawns, scampi, shrimps (all varieties of shrimp), lobster tails	5–6 minutes	Arrange in a ring in a shallow dish
Lobster, crab	6–8 minutes	Cook, covered, in a deep dish. Stand for 5 minutes before serving

CRUNCHY-TOPPED FISH CASSEROLE

Metric/imperial		American
50g/2 oz	butter	½ stick
	1 onion, chopped	
100g/4 oz	button mushrooms	1 cup
	1 green pepper, de-seeded and chopped	
400g/14 oz	chopped canned tomatoes	14 oz
150ml/¼ pint	dry white wine	⅔ cup
	salt, freshly ground pepper	
	4 cod fillets (175–225g/6–8 oz each approx)	
100g/4 oz	freshly made breadcrumbs	2 cups
2×15ml spoons/ 2 tablespoons	chopped parsley	2 tablespoons
1×15ml spoon/ 1 tablespoon	hard cheese, grated	1 tablespoon

Melt half the butter in a large shallow dish for 1 minute on HIGH. Add the onion, and, cook, covered, for 2 minutes on HIGH. Add the mushrooms, pepper, tomatoes, wine, salt and pepper, and stir well. Cook, uncovered, for 5 minutes on HIGH. Add the cod fillets to the dish.

Put the remaining butter into a small bowl, and melt for 1 minute on HIGH. Stir in the breadcrumbs, parsley and cheese, sprinkle the mixture over the fish, and cook on HIGH for 10–12 minutes or until the fish flakes. Brown under a grill (broiler).

COD À L'ORANGE

Metric/imperial		American
	4 cod steaks (total weight 675g/1½ lb approx)	
	grated rind and strained juice of 1 orange	
	salt, freshly ground pepper	
25g/1 oz	butter	2 tablespoons
	GARNISH chopped peanuts	
	orange wedges	

Put the cod steaks into a shallow casserole, the thin ends towards the centre. Pour over the orange juice, sprinkle with the rind and with salt and pepper. Top with flakes of butter. Cook, covered, on HIGH for 6–8 minutes or until the fish flakes. Garnish with chopped peanuts and orange wedges.

Note This quick and easy recipe has a delicious fresh taste.

Chilled Watercress Soup (page 22), Cod à L'Orange **and** Golden Pears (page 59)

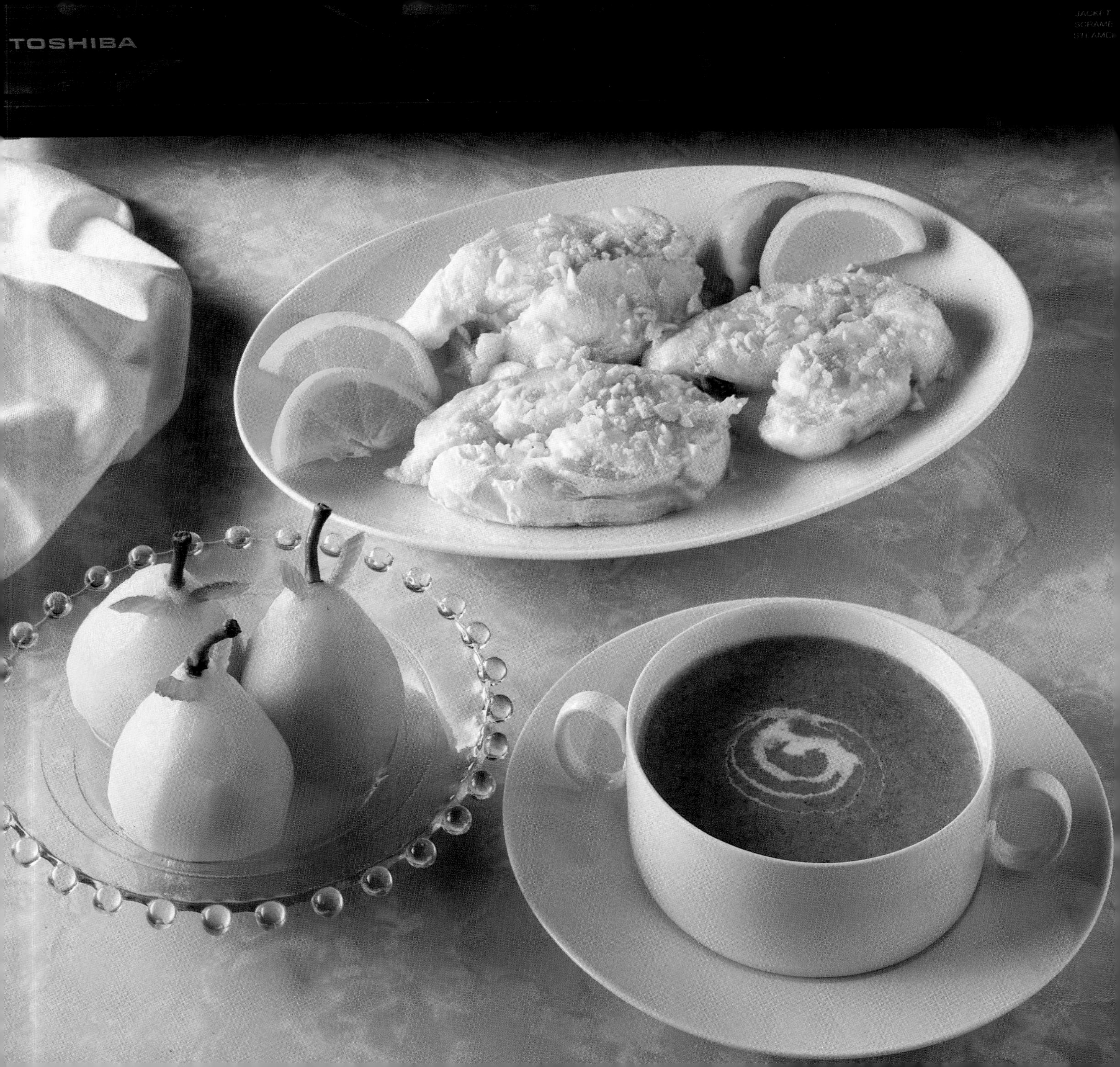
TOSHIBA

PLAICE (FLOUNDER) IN CHEESE AND PRAWN (SHRIMP) SAUCE

Serves 2

Metric/imperial		American
	4 plaice (flounder) fillets, 100–150g/ 4–5 oz each approx, skinned	
	salt, freshly ground white pepper	
	lemon juice	
175g/6 oz	prawns (shrimp), shelled	6 oz
2×5ml spoons/ 2 teaspoons	butter	2 teaspoons
20g/¾ oz	plain (all-purpose) flour	3 tablespoons
	a pinch of mustard powder	
300ml/½ pint	milk	1¼ cups
40g/1½ oz	hard cheese, grated	6 tablespoons
	GARNISH chopped parsley	

Sprinkle the fillets with the salt, pepper and a little lemon juice. Lay three or four prawns (shrimp) on each fillet and roll up. Put the fish into a small round casserole.

Melt the butter for 1 minute on HIGH. Stir in the flour, and cook for 30 seconds on HIGH. Add the mustard, and gradually stir in the milk to form a smooth paste. Heat for 3 minutes on HIGH. Stir on removal from the cooker, add the cheese and the remaining prawns (shrimp). Cook for 2 minutes on HIGH.

Pour the sauce over the fish. Cook, covered, on HIGH for 6 minutes or until the fish flakes. Garnish with parsley.

CURRIED HADDOCK WITH PRAWNS (SHRIMP) AND RICE

Metric/imperial		American
50g/2 oz	butter	½ stick
	6 spring onions (scallions), sliced finely	
2×5ml spoons/ 2 teaspoons	curry powder	2 teaspoons
175g/6 oz	cooked rice	2¼ cups
3×15ml spoons/ 3 tablespoons	dry white wine	3 tablespoons
	3 hard-boiled eggs, chopped	
100g/4 oz	prawns (shrimp), peeled	¼ lb
350g/12 oz	cooked smoked haddock, flaked	¾ lb
	salt, freshly ground pepper	
4×15ml spoons/ 4 tablespoons	double (heavy) cream	¼ cup
	GARNISH 1 hard-boiled egg, sliced	
	paprika	

Melt the butter in a medium casserole for 1 minute on HIGH. Stir in the spring onions (scallions), and cook for 2 minutes on MEDIUM. Stir in the curry powder, rice and wine, and cook, covered, for 5 minutes on HIGH. Stir in the chopped eggs, prawns (shrimp) and haddock. Season to taste. Heat for 8 minutes on HIGH. Stir in the cream. Garnish with the sliced egg, and sprinkle with paprika.

POACHED SALMON CUTLETS (STEAKS)

Metric/imperial		American
	4 salmon cutlets (steaks) (175–225g/ 6–8 oz each, approx)	
2×15ml spoons/ 2 tablespoons	lemon juice	2 tablespoons
2×15ml spoons/ 2 tablespoons	water	2 tablespoons
2×15ml spoons/ 2 tablespoons	white wine	2 tablespoons
	salt, freshly ground pepper	

Put the salmon in a shallow casserole, and sprinkle with the lemon juice, water and wine. Season lightly with salt and pepper. Cook, covered, on MEDIUM for 6–9 minutes or until the fish flakes. Stand until cold.

Remove the fish from the liquid, and serve chilled, with Hollandaise Sauce (page 54).

SCALLOPS IN CIDER

Metric/imperial		American
	4 large scallops, each cut into slices	
150ml/¼ pint	dry cider	⅔ cup
150ml/¼ pint	water	⅔ cup
1×15ml spoon/ 1 tablespoon	lemon juice	1 tablespoon
	1 bay leaf	
25g/1 oz	butter	2 tablespoons
25g/1 oz	flour	¼ cup
100g/4 oz	button mushrooms, sliced	1 cup
	salt, freshly ground pepper	
450g/1 lb	potatoes, cooked and mashed	1 lb
2×15ml spoons/ 2 tablespoons	single (light) cream	2 tablespoons

Put the scallops, cider, water, lemon juice and bay leaf into a medium container. Cook, covered, for 8 minutes on HIGH, then strain and reserve the liquid.

Melt the butter in a separate small dish for 1 minute on HIGH. Stir in the flour. Gradually mix in the reserved liquid. Cook on HIGH for 4–5 minutes or until boiling. Stir once during this cycle and on removal from the cooker. Stir in the mushrooms, scallops and seasoning.

Pipe the mashed potatoes around four scallop shells or small dishes. Brown the potato under a grill (broiler).

Add the cream to the scallop mixture, and heat for 2–3 minutes on HIGH. Fill the shells, and serve.

SEAFOOD PASTA

Metric/imperial		American
1×15ml spoon/ 1 tablespoon	cooking oil	1 tablespoon
	1 onion, finely chopped	
	1 red pepper, de-seeded and chopped	
	1 clove of garlic, chopped	
225g/8 oz	cooked pasta shells	½ lb
1×5ml spoon/ 1 teaspoon	turmeric	1 teaspoon
100g/4 oz	shelled prawns (shrimp)	¼ lb
175g/6 oz	frozen peas	1¼ cups
	1 medium crab, white meat only, chopped	
100g/4 oz	mussels, cooked	¼ lb
	salt, freshly ground black pepper	

Put the oil, onion, red pepper and garlic into a large casserole, and cook, covered, for 5 minutes on MEDIUM. Stir in the pasta and turmeric, and cook for 2 minutes on HIGH. Add the prawns (shrimp), peas, crabmeat and mussels, and season to taste. Heat, covered, for 8 minutes on HIGH. Stir once or twice during this cycle and on removal from the cooker. Serve garnished with the remaining crab claws.

SHRIMP PILAU

Serves 2

Metric/imperial		American
600ml/1 pint	chicken stock	2½ cups
	strained juice and pared rind of 1 lemon	
1×2.5ml spoon/ ½ teaspoon	saffron powder	½ teaspoon
2×15ml spoons/ 2 tablespoons	cooking oil	2 tablespoons
175g/6 oz	long-grain rice	¾ cup
	salt	
75g/3 oz	green beans, cooked and chopped	⅔ cup
75g/3 oz	cooked peas	½ cup
225g/8 oz	shrimps **or** prawns, peeled	½ lb
25g/1 oz	flaked (slivered) almonds, browned	¼ cup

Heat the stock with strips of lemon rind and the saffron powder for 8 minutes on HIGH. Stand for 20 minutes.
Put the oil in a large dish with the rice. Stir well, and heat, covered, for 3 minutes on MEDIUM.
Remove the lemon rind from the stock, then pour it over the rice. Add salt to taste. Cook, covered, for 12 minutes on HIGH. Add the lemon juice, beans, peas and shrimps, and cook, covered, for 8 minutes on HIGH. Stir before serving sprinkled with almonds.

Seafood Pasta

LIGHTER CENTRE PIECES

With imaginative use of vegetables, pasta, rice, nuts, eggs and cheese, a wide variety of meals can be produced quickly in a microwave cooker, the food retaining a high nutritional value, good colour and flavour.

Eggs and cheese both respond very quickly indeed to the microwave energy, so it is important to take care when cooking them. Always use eggs at room temperature rather than taken from the refrigerator, and remember to prick yolks before using them in the cooker, and not to boil eggs in their shells.

Take care not to overcook cheese as it can become stringy and hard. Cheese is generally added during the last few minutes of the cooking time. Do not attempt to re-heat any egg dishes in a microwave cooker as the eggs tend to toughen and overcook. If re-heating a dish topped with cheese, add this just before re-heating, and not during the original cooking time.

For rice and pasta, follow the cooking chart below.

Rice and Pasta Cooking Chart

Cook all rice and pasta in boiling salted water in a large covered container. The timing starts as soon as the food is added to the water. Stir once or twice during the cooking time.

	Quantity	Water	Time	Standing time
Rice type				
Long-grain	225g/8 oz/1 US cup	600ml/1 pint/2½ US cups	10 minutes	10 minutes
Brown rice	225g/8 oz/1 US cup	600ml/1 pint/2½ US cups	25–30 minutes	10 minutes
Pasta type				
Noodles/tagliatelle (Fettuccine)	225g/8 oz/1 US cup	900ml/1½ pints/3¾ US cups	6–8 minutes	5 minutes
Macaroni	225g/8 oz/1 US cup	900ml/1½ pints/3¾ US cups	10–12 minutes	5 minutes
Pasta shapes and shells	225g/8 oz/1 US cup	900ml/1½ pints/3¾ US cups	12–14 minutes	8 minutes
Spaghetti	225g/8 oz/1 US cup	900ml/1½ pints/3¾ US cups	14–16 minutes	8 minutes
Lasagne (use an oblong dish)	225g/8 oz/1 US cup	900ml/1½ pints/3¾ US cups	14–16 minutes	8 minutes

Note Cooking times etc for other pasta types can be gauged by their similarity with the principal types listed above.

VEGETABLE LASAGNE

Metric/imperial		American
	1 onion, thinly sliced	
	1 green pepper, de-seeded and sliced finely	
225g/8 oz	carrots, diced	1½ cups
	3 stalks celery, sliced thinly	
150ml/¼ pint	vegetable stock	⅔ cup
225g/8 oz	tomatoes, skinned and sliced	½ lb
225g/8 oz	canned whole kernel sweetcorn, drained	1½ cups
40g/1½ oz	butter	3 tablespoons
40g/1½ oz	flour	6 tablespoons
450ml/¾ pint	milk	2 cups
	10 sheets dry packeted lasagne verde, cooked (page 42)	
225g/8 oz	hard cheese, grated	2 cups
	plain crisps (potato chips), crushed (optional)	

Put the onion, pepper, carrots, celery and vegetable stock into a large casserole. Cook, covered, for 10 minutes on HIGH. Stir in the tomatoes and sweetcorn, and cook, covered, for a further 5 minutes on HIGH.

Melt the butter in a medium basin (bowl) on HIGH for 1 minute. Stir in the flour, and cook on HIGH for 1 minute. Stir in the milk gradually. Cook for 5 minutes on HIGH, stirring half-way through this cycle and at the end of the cooking time.

Pour a layer of the sauce into a large shallow dish, cover with a layer of the lasagne, then a layer of the mixed vegetables topped with the cheese. Repeat the layering, finishing with a layer of cheese. Cook, covered, for 12–15 minutes on HIGH.

If the dish is ovenproof, brown under a grill (broiler), otherwise sprinkle with the crushed crisps (potato chips).

EGG LAYER CRISP

Serves 2

Metric/imperial		American
100g/4 oz	butter	1 stick
25g/1 oz	flour	¼ cup
300ml/½ pint	milk	1¼ cups
	salt, freshly ground black pepper	
	4 hard-boiled eggs, chopped	
150g/5 oz	freshly made breadcrumbs	2½ cups

Melt 25g/1 oz/2 US tablespoons butter in a medium bowl for 1 minute on HIGH. Add the flour, and mix well, then cook for 1 minute on HIGH. Heat the milk for 2 minutes on HIGH, then gradually stir it into the flour, and mix until smooth. Return to the cooker for 2 minutes on HIGH. Stir in the seasoning and the eggs, and cook for 2 minutes on HIGH.

Melt the remaining butter in a shallow dish for 2 minutes on HIGH. Mix in the breadcrumbs, and heat for 10–15 minutes on HIGH, stirring with a fork several times until browned evenly.

Place a layer of breadcrumb mixture in a dish, cover with the egg mixture, and top with the remaining breadcrumbs. Heat in the cooker for 3 minutes on HIGH. Serve immediately.

Variation
Substitute 200g/7 oz chopped canned salmon for the eggs.

LEEK AND TOMATO MACARONI CHEESE

Metric/imperial		American
900ml/1½ pints	boiling water	1 quart
	3 medium leeks, cleaned and cut into chunks	
175g/6 oz	elbow macaroni	1½ cups
	salt, freshly ground pepper	
175g/6 oz	hard cheese, grated	1½ cups
300ml/½ pint	milk	1¼ cups
	2 eggs, beaten	
1×5ml spoon/ 1 teaspoon	prepared English mustard	1 teaspoon
225g/8 oz	tomatoes, skinned and chopped	½ lb
	GARNISH grated cheese (optional)	
	plain crisps (potato chips), crushed (optional)	

Put the boiling water, leeks, macaroni and a little salt into a large casserole. Cook, covered, on HIGH for 15 minutes or until the macaroni is just tender. Drain off the liquid, and blend with the cheese, milk, eggs, mustard and salt and pepper. Heat for 12 minutes on HIGH, stirring half-way through the cycle. Add the chopped tomatoes.

Turn the macaroni and leeks into a shallow serving dish, and heat, uncovered, for a further 8 minutes on HIGH.

If the dish is ovenproof, sprinkle with a little additional grated cheese, and brown under the grill (broiler); otherwise sprinkle with the crushed crisps (potato chips).

BROWN RICE RING

Metric/imperial		American
600ml/1 pint	boiling water	2½ cups
225g/8 oz	brown rice	1 cup
1×5ml spoon/ 1 teaspoon	salt	1 teaspoon
25g/1 oz	butter	2 tablespoons
	1 medium onion, chopped finely	
	2 stalks celery, chopped finely	
200g/7 oz	canned whole kernel sweetcorn, drained	scant 1½ cups
2×15ml spoons/ 2 tablespoons	chopped parsley	2 tablespoons

Pour the water into a large casserole, and add the rice and salt. Cook, covered, on HIGH for 25–30 minutes or until the rice is tender. Stand for 10 minutes before draining.

Melt the butter in a medium casserole for 1 minute on HIGH, stir in the onion and celery, and cook for 3 minutes on HIGH. Add the sweetcorn and parsley, and heat for 3 minutes on HIGH.

Stir the vegetables into the rice, and check the seasoning. Turn the rice into a greased medium microwave cake ring. Heat, covered, for 5 minutes on HIGH, then turn out immediately.

Brown Rice Ring

GREEN BEAN AND TOMATO CASSEROLE

Metric/imperial		American
450g/1 lb	potatoes, sliced thinly	1 lb
4×15ml spoons/ 4 tablespoons	milk	¼ cup
	1 onion, chopped finely	
	1 red pepper, de-seeded and sliced	
	1 green pepper, de-seeded and sliced	
1×15ml spoon/ 1 tablespoon	cooking oil	1 tablespoon
450g/1 lb	whole green beans, cooked	1 lb
400g/14 oz	chopped canned tomatoes	14 oz
150ml/¼ pint	stock	⅔ cup
2×5ml spoons/ 2 teaspoons	Worcestershire sauce	2 teaspoons
	salt, freshly ground pepper	
1×15ml spoon/ 1 tablespoon	chopped parsley	1 tablespoon
	3 rashers (slices) bacon, rinds removed and chopped	

Put the potatoes into a shallow casserole, pour the milk on top, and cover. Cook for 8 minutes on HIGH.

Put the onion with the red and green peppers into a medium casserole. Add the oil, and cook, covered, for 5 minutes on HIGH. Blend the pepper mixture with the beans, tomatoes, stock, Worcestershire sauce, salt and pepper.

Arrange the vegetable mixture over the potatoes, and scatter with the parsley. Cook, covered, for 15 minutes on HIGH.

Cook the bacon on a roasting rack or absorbent paper (paper towels) for 4½ minutes on HIGH or until crisp. Allow to cool slightly, then crumble, and sprinkle over the top of the casserole.

BAKED POTATOES WITH CREAM CHEESE AND BACON CRUMBLE

Metric/imperial		American
	4 potatoes (225g/8 oz each approx), pricked or scored	
	4 rashers (slices) streaky bacon, rinds removed and chopped	
75g/3 oz	cream cheese	3 oz
1×15ml spoon/ 1 tablespoon	chopped chives	1 tablespoon
	salt, freshly ground pepper	

Wrap the potatoes in absorbent paper (paper towels), and cook for approximately 12–16 minutes on HIGH depending on the size and type of potato.

Cook the bacon on a roasting rack or absorbent paper (paper towels) for 3–5 minutes on HIGH until crisp. Allow to cool slightly, then crumble.

Soften the cream cheese in a small bowl for 30–45 seconds on MEDIUM. Stir in the chives and seasoning.

Slit the potatoes, put some cheese mixture in each, and sprinkle with the bacon.

STUFFED AUBERGINES (EGGPLANTS)

Metric/imperial		American
	4 medium aubergines (eggplants)	
	1 onion, chopped finely	
	1 carrot, chopped finely	
2 × 15ml spoons/ 2 tablespoons	cooking oil	2 tablespoons
50g/2 oz	walnuts, chopped	$\frac{1}{2}$ cup
100g/4 oz	hard cheese, grated	1 cup
2 × 15ml spoons/ 2 tablespoons	oats, flaked (rolled oats)	2 tablespoons
	salt, freshly ground pepper	
150ml/$\frac{1}{4}$ pint	vegetable stock	$\frac{2}{3}$ cup
	GARNISH grated white cabbage	
	cress	

Cut a thick slice lengthways from each aubergine (eggplant), and remove the pulp, leaving the shells about 6mm/$\frac{1}{4}$ inch thick. Chop the pulp, then mix with the onion and carrot.

Heat the oil for 30 seconds on HIGH. Stir in the aubergine (eggplant) mixture. Cook, covered, for 4 minutes on HIGH. Add the nuts, cheese, oats and seasoning. Fill the aubergine (eggplant) shells with this mixture. Arrange the aubergines (eggplants) in a shallow casserole, and add the vegetable stock. Cook, covered, on HIGH for 15 minutes or until the aubergine (eggplant) shells are soft. Garnish with white cabbage and cress.

CHINESE MEDLEY

Serves 2

Metric/imperial		American
2 × 5ml spoons/ 2 teaspoons	sunflower oil	2 teaspoons
	1 small onion, sliced finely	
	1 stalk of celery, sliced finely	
	1 green pepper, de-seeded and sliced finely	
75g/3 oz	button mushrooms, sliced	$\frac{3}{4}$ cup
1 × 15ml spoon/ 1 tablespoon	cornflour (cornstarch)	1 tablespoon
2 × 15ml spoons/ 2 tablespoons	light soy sauce	2 tablespoons
1 × 15ml spoon/ 1 tablespoon	dry sherry	1 tablespoon
150ml/$\frac{1}{4}$ pint	water	$\frac{2}{3}$ cup
100g/4 oz	beansprouts	1 cup
25g/1 oz	toasted almonds	$\frac{1}{4}$ cup

Heat the oil in a large shallow dish for 30 seconds on HIGH. Add the onion, celery and green pepper. Coat well with the oil, and cook for 3 minutes on HIGH. Stir in the mushrooms. Cook for 2 minutes on HIGH.

Blend the cornflour (cornstarch) with the soy sauce, sherry and water until smooth. Stir this mixture into the vegetables, and cook for 3 minutes on HIGH. Stir in the beansprouts and toasted almonds. Cook for a further 6 minutes on HIGH before serving.

DOLMADES

Metric/imperial		American
225g/8 oz	vine (grape) leaves in brine (see **Note**)	8 oz
225g/8 oz	rice, cooked	3 cups
	½ onion, chopped finely	
	salt, freshly ground pepper	
2×5ml spoons/ 2 teaspoons	finely chopped mint	2 teaspoons
7×15ml spoons/ 7 tablespoons	concentrated tomato purée (paste)	½ cup
	vegetable stock	

Lay the vine (grape) leaves out flat. Mix together the rice, onion, salt, pepper and mint. Put 1×5ml spoon/1 teaspoon of the mixture into each leaf, fold up into a parcel, and squeeze gently in the hand. Arrange in a dish, taking care that the rolls are not too tightly packed. Mix the tomato purée (paste) with enough stock to yield 450ml/¾ pint/2 US cups liquid. Cook, covered, for 15 minutes on HIGH. Leave to cool, then chill before serving.

Note Rinse the vine (grape) leaves in cold water, and drain well before using.

CHEESY VEGETABLES

Metric/imperial		American
550g/1¼ lb	potatoes, thinly sliced	1¼ lb
	salt, freshly ground pepper	
	1 large onion, thinly sliced	
225g/8 oz	hard cheese, grated	2 cups
300ml/½ pint	milk	1¼ cups
50g/2 oz	butter	½ stick
225g/8 oz	tomatoes, sliced	½ lb

Put a layer of potatoes into a shallow dish, and add seasoning. Spread with the onion, and sprinkle with half of the cheese. Cover with the remaining potatoes, add seasoning, and top with the remaining cheese. Pour over the milk, and dot with the butter. Cook, covered, for 25 minutes on HIGH. Cover with the sliced tomatoes. Heat, uncovered, on HIGH for 8 minutes or until the potatoes are cooked. Stand for 5 minutes before serving.

If the dish is ovenproof, brown under a grill (broiler).

Note This can be served with hot or cold meat, and also fish.

Accompaniments

Vegetables cooked in a microwave cooker retain all their natural flavour and colour. Very little or no water is required; indeed, some vegetables such as frozen peas are cooked without any at all. Sauces are made in minutes and rarely become lumpy or, in the case of delicate sauces, curdle.

If preparing vegetable dishes in advance, undercook slightly as there will be further cooking during the re-heating period. If heating vegetables in a sauce, heat the vegetables first, then the sauce and combine the two before serving.

Remember that salt should be added *after* cooking as it can cause spot dehydration of the vegetables if added beforehand. Taste before seasoning as the natural flavour is stronger than usual.

Pulses (Legumes)

Dried beans, peas and lentils can be cooked in a microwave cooker, but as with conventional methods, they require soaking overnight in cold water. Dried beans must then be drained thoroughly, and boiled briskly in fresh water for at least 10 minutes.

To cook, place 225g/8 oz/1¼ US cups pulses (legumes) into a large container. Cover with 1.5 litres/2½ pints/1¼ US quarts boiling water. Cover, and cook on HIGH for 10 minutes, then on MEDIUM for 1–2 hours, depending on variety. Be prepared to top up the water level with boiling water from a kettle, as and when required.

Vegetable Cooking Chart

Put the prepared vegetables into a dish with water, cover, and cook for the suggested time (see below). Stir once or twice where possible during the cycle. Stand, covered, on removal from the cooker (see below), then drain and season before serving. All timings are for a firm finish, so longer or shorter cooking periods may be needed to suit personal preference.

All weights are 450g/1 lb unless otherwise specified.

Group	Preparation	Water	Cooking time on HIGH	Standing time
Leaves, eg Spinach	Wash but do not dry	None	5–7 minutes	3 minutes
Cabbage family White cabbage	Shred and put in a large dish	150ml/¼ pint/⅔ US cup	8–10 minutes	5 minutes
Cauliflower	Florets	150ml/¼ pint/⅔ US cup	15–18 minutes	7 minutes
	Whole	150ml/¼ pint/⅔ US cup	15–18 minutes	7 minutes

Chart continues over.

Group	Preparation	Water	Cooking time on HIGH	Standing time
Brussels sprouts	Cut large sprouts in half	8×15ml spoons/ 8 tablespoons/½ US cup	10–11 minutes	5 minutes
Broccoli	Put in a shallow dish, head to stalk	150ml/¼ pint/⅔ US cup	10–12 minutes	5 minutes
Roots and tubers Carrots	Chunks or quarter whole carrots	150ml/¼ pint/⅔ US cup	8–10 minutes	8 minutes
Potatoes	Quarter	150ml/¼ pint/⅔ US cup	10–12 minutes	5 minutes
Baby new potatoes	Whole	150ml/¼ pint/⅔ US cup	10–12 minutes	5 minutes
Jacket (baking) potatoes	Wrap in absorbent paper (paper towels)	None	5–7 minutes	Wrap in foil. Will keep hot up to 20 minutes
Pods and seeds Peas	Shell	150ml/¼ pint/⅔ US cup	10–12 minutes	5 minutes
French (green) beans	Top and tail	150ml/¼ pint/⅔ US cup	13–15 minutes	5 minutes
Corn–on–the–cob	Cook in husk or remove	4×15ml spoons/ 4 tablespoons/¼ US cup	4–6 minutes	5 minutes
Vegetable fruits Tomatoes	Halve	None. Use knob of butter	2 tomatoes 1½–2 minutes	2 minutes
Squashes Courgettes (zucchini)	Whole	4×15ml spoons/ 4 tablespoons/¼ US cup	6–8 minutes	5 minutes
	Slice	4×15ml spoons/ 4 tablespoons/¼ US cup	5–7 minutes	3 minutes
Stalks and shoots Asparagus	Put in a shallow dish, top to tail	6×15ml spoons/ 6 tablespoons	12–14 minutes	5 minutes
Onion family 4 onions	Peel	6×15ml spoons/ 6 tablespoons	10–12 minutes	5 minutes

Many suppliers of frozen vegetables give suggested microwave cooking times and amounts of water on the packets. As a general rule, add 4×15ml spoons/4 tablespoons/¼ US cup per 450g/1 lb of vegetables, and cook for a quarter less time than fresh. Brussels sprouts will, however, take longer.

BROCCOLI AMANDINE

Metric/imperial		American
450g/1 lb	fresh broccoli, stalks halved lengthways	1 lb
150ml/¼ pint	water	⅔ cup
40g/1½ oz	butter	3 tablespoons
40g/1½ oz	flaked (slivered) almonds	6 tablespoons
1×15ml spoon/ 1 tablespoon	lemon juice	1 tablespoon
	salt, freshly ground pepper	

Put the broccoli, head to stalk, in a shallow dish. Add the water, cover, and cook for 10–12 minutes on HIGH.

Put the butter and the flaked (slivered) almonds in a small shallow dish. Cook for 3–5 minutes on HIGH, stirring often to ensure the almonds are browned evenly. Add the lemon juice, salt and pepper.

Drain the broccoli, and pour the butter and almonds on top. Return to the cooker for 3 minutes on HIGH before serving.

FRENCH STYLE PETITS POIS

Metric/imperial		American
25g/1 oz	butter	2 tablespoons
450g/1 lb	petits pois, frozen	1 lb
	1 onion, finely sliced	
1×15ml spoon/ 1 tablespoon	chopped parsley	1 tablespoon
	1 sprig of thyme	
1×5ml spoon/ 1 teaspoon	caster (superfine) sugar	1 teaspoon
	1 lettuce heart, shredded	
2×15ml spoons/ 2 tablespoons	water	2 tablespoons
	salt, freshly ground pepper	

Melt the butter in a medium casserole for 1 minute on HIGH. Stir in the petits pois, onion, parsley and thyme. Heat, covered, for 5 minutes on HIGH. Stir half-way through the cycle. Stir in the sugar, lettuce and water, and cook, covered, for 6 minutes on HIGH. Leave to stand for 5 minutes. Season to taste before serving.

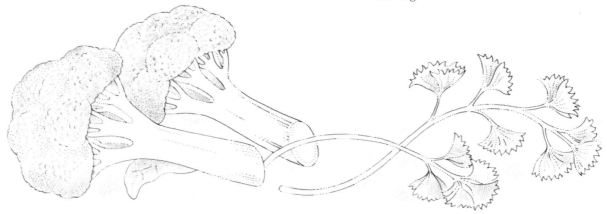

COURGETTES (ZUCCHINI) IN LEMON SAUCE

Metric/imperial		American
350g/12 oz	courgettes (zucchini) cut into quarters lengthways	¾ lb
6×15ml spoons/ 6 tablespoons	water	6 tablespoons
225ml/8 fl oz (approx)	chicken stock	1 cup
25g/1 oz	butter	2 tablespoons
25g/1 oz	flour	¼ cup
2× size 2	egg yolks	2 large
2×15ml spoons/ 2 tablespoons	lemon juice	2 tablespoons
	salt, freshly ground white pepper	
	GARNISH chopped parsley	

Put the courgettes (zucchini) into a medium dish with the water. Cook, covered, on HIGH for 12–15 minutes or until just soft. Remove from the cooker. Drain off the liquid, and make up to 300ml/½ pint/1¼ US cups with the chicken stock.

Melt the butter in a small container for 1 minute on HIGH. Stir in the flour, and cook for 30 seconds on HIGH. Gradually add the stock, whisking well. Cook on HIGH for 4–5 minutes or until the stock begins to boil. Stir once during this cycle and on removal from the cooker. Cool slightly, then whisk in the egg yolks, lemon juice and seasoning.

Pour the sauce over the courgettes (zucchini), and heat for 2 minutes on HIGH. Garnish with parsley.

Use with poultry, pork and fish.

BROAD (FAVA) BEANS AND ARTICHOKES

Metric/imperial		American
450g/1 lb	broad (fava) beans, fresh **or** frozen	1 lb
3×15ml spoons/ 3 tablespoons	water	3 tablespoons
2×5ml spoons/ 2 teaspoons	cornflour (cornstarch)	2 teaspoons
1×15ml spoon/ 1 tablespoon	cooking oil	1 tablespoon
	salt, freshly ground pepper	
1×15ml spoon/ 1 tablespoon	chopped parsley	1 tablespoon
425g/15 oz	canned artichoke hearts	15 oz

Put the broad (fava) beans in a medium container with the water, and cook, covered, for 10 minutes on HIGH.

Mix the cornflour (cornstarch) with the oil until smooth, pour in the strained bean water, and stir well. Add the seasoning, parsley, artichoke hearts and their liquid and the beans. Stir, then heat for 5 minutes on HIGH. Stir before serving.

Apricot Hock (page 31) **and** Courgettes (Zucchini) in Lemon Sauce

HOLLANDAISE SAUCE

Metric/imperial		American
2×15ml spoons/ 2 tablespoons	wine vinegar	2 tablespoons
1×15ml spoon/ 1 tablespoon	water	1 tablespoon
100g/4 oz	butter	1 stick
	2 egg yolks	
	salt, freshly ground pepper	

Put the vinegar and water in a small bowl, and cook for 2 minutes on HIGH. Stir in the butter. Beat in the egg yolks and seasoning. Cook on MEDIUM for 1½–3 minutes or until the sauce has thickened. Whisk once or twice during this cycle and on removal from the cooker. Watch the sauce carefully to make sure that it does not overcook.

VELOUTÉ SAUCE

Metric/imperial		American
25g/1 oz	butter	2 tablespoons
2×15ml spoons/ 2 tablespoons	flour	2 tablespoons
450ml/¾ pint	chicken stock	2 cups
3×15ml spoons/ 3 tablespoons	single (light) cream	3 tablespoons
	a few drops lemon juice	
	salt, freshly ground white pepper	

Melt the butter in a medium bowl for 30 seconds on HIGH. Stir in the flour, and cook for 30 seconds on HIGH. Stir in the stock gradually, return to the cooker, and cook for 8 minutes on HIGH, stirring or whisking every 2 minutes. Remove from the cooker, stir again, then add the cream, lemon juice and seasoning.

BARBECUE SAUCE

Metric/imperial		American
1×15ml spoon/ 1 tablespoon	vegetable oil	1 tablespoon
	1 large onion, finely chopped	
2×15ml spoons/ 2 tablespoons	concentrated tomato purée (paste)	2 tablespoons
2×15ml spoons/ 2 tablespoons	Worcestershire sauce	2 tablespoons
2×15ml spoons/ 2 tablespoons	soft brown sugar	2 tablespoons
2×5ml spoons/ 2 teaspoons	mustard powder	2 teaspoons
150ml/¼ pint	warm water	⅔ cup

Put the oil into a small bowl, add the onion, and cook, covered, for 5–6 minutes on MEDIUM. Stir in the tomato purée (paste), and cook, uncovered, for 1 minute on HIGH.

Blend the Worcestershire sauce, sugar and mustard powder with the warm water in a basin (bowl). Add to the onion mixture, and blend well. Cook, uncovered, for 6 minutes on HIGH, stirring after 3 minutes and on removal from the cooker.

Note Serve this sauce with hamburgers and other meat dishes, both hot and cold.

Sweet Dreams

No matter whether they are light or heavy, puddings and desserts are both quick and easy to make in a microwave cooker.

Do, however, watch fruit carefully during the cooking time as it can soften rapidly and lose its shape. Use MEDIUM power for greater control and for a better flavour from the juices which penetrate the fruit.

Egg sauces and delicate chocolate sauces are particularly easy to make in the cooker, as they require very little watching. They should be heated, and cooked on MEDIUM to prevent any chance of overcooking.

Use the cooker also to re-heat fruit pies cooked conventionally. A pie with shortcrust pastry heats better than one made with flaky or puff pastry. Christmas puddings re-heat perfectly, but timings should be kept short and progress checked. A 450g/1 lb pudding will heat on HIGH in under 5 minutes.

Baked Bananas

Metric/imperial		American
	4 bananas, peeled	
3×15ml spoons/ 3 tablespoons	soft brown sugar	3 tablespoons
1×5ml spoon/ 1 teaspoon	ground cinnamon	1 teaspoon
4×15ml spoons/ 4 tablespoons	ginger wine	$\frac{1}{4}$ cup
50g/2 oz	flaked hazelnuts	$\frac{1}{2}$ cup

Put the bananas in a shallow dish. Mix the sugar with the cinnamon, and sprinkle over the bananas. Pour over the ginger wine, and heat, uncovered, on MEDIUM for 8 minutes. Sprinkle with the hazelnuts.

Serve with whipped cream.

RASPBERRY FLAN (TART)

Metric/imperial		American
25g/1 oz	wholewheat flour	$\frac{1}{4}$ cup
75g/3 oz	plain (all-purpose) flour	$\frac{3}{4}$ cup
50g/2 oz	butter	$\frac{1}{2}$ stick
	1 egg yolk	
2×15ml spoons/ 2 tablespoons	water	2 tablespoons
350g/12 oz	whole raspberries	3 cups
2×15ml spoons/ 2 tablespoons	redcurrant jelly	2 tablespoons
2×15ml spoons/ 2 tablespoons	red wine	2 tablespoons
	CUSTARD FILLING	
1× size 3	egg	1 medium
25g/1 oz	caster (superfine) sugar	2 tablespoons
1×15ml spoon/ 1 tablespoon	plain (all-purpose) flour	1 tablespoon
300ml/$\frac{1}{2}$ pint	milk	$1\frac{1}{4}$ cups

Mix together the flours, and rub in the butter until it resembles fine breadcrumbs. Bind with the egg yolk and water. Roll out on a floured surface, and use to line a 20cm/8 inch greased flan dish (tart pan). Cover the pastry with a sheet of greaseproof (waxed) paper or layering tissue (tissue paper), and cover with dried beans. Chill in a refrigerator for 10 minutes, then cook for 3 minutes on HIGH. Remove the beans and paper, and cook for a further 1–2 minutes on HIGH. Leave to cool.

To make the filling, whisk together the egg, sugar, flour and 2×15ml spoons/2 tablespoons of the milk. Heat the remaining milk in a jug (measuring cup) for 2 minutes on HIGH, pour into the mixture, and heat for 5 minutes on MEDIUM. Stir half-way through this cycle and on removal from the cooker. Cook until the custard thickens. Leave to cool, then pour on to the pastry base.

Arrange the raspberries on the custard filling. Heat the redcurrant jelly and wine for 1$\frac{1}{2}$ minutes on HIGH. Cool, then use to glaze the flan (tart).

SUMMER FLUFF

Serves 2

Metric/imperial		American
350g/12 oz	soft fruits (eg raspberries, redcurrants, strawberries)	3 cups
50ml/2 fl oz	red wine	scant $\frac{1}{4}$ cup
2–4×15ml spoons/2–4 tablespoons	icing (confectioner's) sugar	2–4 tablespoons
	1 egg white	
25g/1 oz	caster (superfine) sugar	2 tablespoons
15g/$\frac{1}{2}$ oz	hazelnuts, chopped	2 tablespoons

Put the fruit in a small serving dish. Pour over the wine, and sweeten to taste with the icing (confectioner's) sugar. Leave to stand for 1 hour.

Whisk the egg white until stiff. Fold in the caster (superfine) sugar. Spread this mixture over the fruit. Heat on HIGH for 2–3 minutes until the topping is firm and risen. Sprinkle with the nuts, and serve at once.

Variation
If making this dessert for children, omit the wine and add 2–3 scoops of ice cream. Cover with the topping and it will make a creamy sauce.

Raspberry Flan (Tart) **and** Pineapple and Orange Meringue Flan (Tart) (page 58)

PINEAPPLE AND ORANGE MERINGUE FLAN (TART)

Metric/imperial		American
40g/1½ oz	butter	3 tablespoons
100g/4 oz	digestive biscuits (graham crackers), crushed finely	scant 1 cup
FILLING		
2 × 15ml spoons/ 2 tablespoons	cornflour (cornstarch)	2 tablespoons
7 × 15ml spoons/ 7 tablespoons	orange juice, strained	½ cup
50g/2 oz	sugar	¼ cup
1 × 5ml spoon/ 1 teaspoon	lemon rind, grated	1 teaspoon
225g/8 oz	canned crushed pineapple	8 oz
	2 egg yolks	
MERINGUE TOPPING		
	2 egg whites	
50g/2 oz	caster (superfine) sugar	¼ cup

Melt the butter in a small bowl for 1½ minutes on HIGH. Mix with the biscuit (cracker) crumbs, and press into the base and sides of a 20cm/8 inch ovenproof flan dish (tart pan). Chill in a refrigerator.

To make the filling, mix the cornflour (cornstarch) with a little of the orange juice to make a smooth paste. Stir in the remaining orange juice gradually, with the sugar, lemon rind, pineapple and egg yolks. Heat for 5–6 minutes on HIGH, stirring every 2 minutes. Remove the mixture from the cooker when it begins to thicken. Mix well, and leave to cool, then fill into the crumb base.

To make the meringue topping, beat the egg whites until soft peaks form, then add the sugar gradually, and beat well. Spoon the meringue over the filling, and brown under a grill (broiler). Serve at once.

APRICOTS WITH CREAMY YOGHURT SAUCE

Serves 2

Metric/imperial		American
225g/8 oz	fresh apricots, halved and stoned (pitted)	½ lb
25g/1 oz	soft brown sugar	2 tablespoons
2 × 15ml spoons/ 2 tablespoons	double (heavy) cream	2 tablespoons
7 × 15ml spoons/ 7 tablespoons	plain yoghurt	½ cup
2 × 15ml spoons/ 2 tablespoons	Demerara (light brown) sugar	2 tablespoons

Put the apricots in a small dish with the soft brown sugar. Cook, covered, on MEDIUM for 6–8 minutes or until the apricots are softened.

Mix together the cream and the yoghurt, and pour this over the apricots. Sprinkle with the Demerara (light brown) sugar, and leave to stand for 5 minutes – this allows the sugar to melt a little. Serve hot or chilled, with sponge (lady) fingers.

GOLDEN PEARS

Metric/imperial		American
300ml/½ pint	orange juice	1¼ cups
150ml/¼ pint	dry white wine	⅔ cup
50g/2 oz	caster (superfine) sugar	¼ cup
	4 pears, peeled stalks *not* removed	
	DECORATION angelica leaves	

Heat the orange juice, wine and sugar in a medium casserole on HIGH for 5 minutes or until all the sugar has dissolved. Add the pears, then cook, covered, on MEDIUM for 20–25 minutes or until the fruit is tender. Leave to cool in the syrup.

Serve cold, decorated with angelica leaves.

Note The cooking time depends on the type and ripeness of the pears.

Variation
A few drops of lemon or orange colouring can be added to the liquid.

STUFFED PEACHES

Metric/imperial		American
50g/2 oz	rich shortcake biscuits (butter cookies), crumbled	⅔ cup
25g/1 oz	ground almonds	¼ cup
1 × 15ml spoon/ 1 tablespoon	white wine	1 tablespoon
1 × 15ml spoon/ 1 tablespoon	apricot jam	1 tablespoon
1 × 5ml spoon/ 1 teaspoon	lemon rind, grated	1 teaspoon
	4 large ripe peaches, skinned and halved (see **Note**)	
	SAUCE	
4 × 15ml spoons/ 4 tablespoons	dry white wine	¼ cup
2 × 15ml spoons/ 2 tablespoons	apricot jam, sieved	2 tablespoons
	DECORATION blanched almonds	

Mix the biscuits (cookies) and ground almonds with the wine, apricot jam and lemon rind. Put a quarter of this mixture into four of the peach halves. Cover with the remaining halves, and arrange in a 20cm/8 inch diameter dish.

To make the sauce, blend the wine and apricot jam, and heat for 30 seconds on HIGH. Pour the sauce over the peaches, and heat on MEDIUM for 6–7 minutes or until the biscuit (cookie) mixture begins to bubble out of the fruit. Baste with a little of the syrup after the first 2 minutes. Serve hot or cold, decorated with a few blanched almonds.

Note To skin peaches easily, heat on HIGH for approximately 2 minutes (for four).

Oranges in Grand Marnier Syrup

Metric/imperial		American
	6 oranges	
100g/4 oz	caster (superfine) sugar	½ cup
	water	
2×15ml spoons/ 2 tablespoons	Grand Marnier	2 tablespoons

Using a serrated knife, peel four of the oranges, and remove the outer membrane. Leave whole, and arrange in a serving dish. Pare the remaining oranges, and cut the rind into thin strips. Squeeze the oranges and strain the juice.

Put the sugar and 7×15ml spoons/7 tablespoons/½ US cup water into a small heat-resistant bowl, heat for 5 minutes on MEDIUM, and stir to dissolve the sugar. Heat on HIGH for 10 minutes or until the liquid has turned golden-brown. Watch this carefully to ensure it does not burn. Add the orange juice to the sugar syrup, stir, and return to the cooker for 20 seconds on HIGH. Stir in the Grand Marnier, and pour this over the oranges. Leave on one side.

Put the orange rind into 150ml/¼ pint/⅔ US cup water, and boil on HIGH for 10 minutes or until soft. Drain, and sprinkle it over the oranges. Leave to cool for several hours before serving, basting the fruit occasionally during this time.

Dried Fruit Compôte

Metric/imperial		American
100g/4 oz	dried apricots	¾ cup
100g/4 oz	dried peaches	¾ cup
100g/4 oz	dried apples	1¼ cups
100g/4 oz	prunes	10 large
450ml/¾ pint	water	2 cups
6×15ml spoons/ 6 tablespoons	clear honey	6 tablespoons
	thinly pared rind of 1 lemon	
4×15ml spoons/ 4 tablespoons	dry sherry	¼ cup

Put the dried fruits and water in a medium dish. Heat, covered, for 10 minutes on HIGH. Stir in the honey, lemon rind and sherry. Heat, covered, for 10 minutes on HIGH, then stand, covered, for 2 hours. Remove the lemon rind. Serve hot or chilled, with plain yoghurt.

Oranges in Grand Marnier Syrup

CHOCOLATE CHEESECAKE

Metric/imperial		American
50g/2 oz	butter	$\frac{1}{2}$ stick
50g/2 oz	granulated sugar	$\frac{1}{4}$ cup
225g/8 oz	semi-sweet biscuits (graham crackers), crushed	$1\frac{3}{4}$ cups
450g/1 lb	cream cheese	1 lb
50g/2 oz	caster (superfine) sugar	$\frac{1}{4}$ cup
3× size 2	eggs	3 large
75g/3 oz	plain (semi-sweet) chocolate	3 squares
	DECORATION whipped cream	
	grated chocolate	

Melt the butter in a medium bowl for $1\frac{1}{2}$ minutes on HIGH. Stir in the granulated sugar and biscuits (cracker crumbs). Line the base of a 22.5cm/9 inch shallow dish with layering tissue (tissue paper). Press the biscuit (crumble) mixture down firmly on to the base of the dish, leaving enough space all round for the cheesecake to be lifted out by the edges of the tissue.

Heat the cheese for 1 minute on MEDIUM. Beat in the caster (superfine) sugar and eggs. Put the chocolate in a small bowl, and heat for 3–4 minutes on MEDIUM, stirring every minute. Stir into the egg and cheese mixture, and pour on to the biscuit (crumb) base. Cook on HIGH for 2–3 minutes or until the edges are just beginning to cook. Turn the cooker down to MEDIUM, and cook for 10–15 minutes or until the centre is set. Leave to cool. Lift the cooled cheesecake carefully out of the dish, and slide on to a plate. Decorate with whipped cream and grated chocolate.

EGG CUSTARD BRÛLÉE

Metric/imperial		American
400g/14 oz	canned evaporated milk	14 oz
4× size 2	eggs	4 large
25g/1 oz	caster (superfine) sugar	2 tablespoons
	a few drops vanilla essence (extract)	
100g/4 oz	light brown sugar	$\frac{1}{2}$ cup

Mix water with the evaporated milk to make up to 300ml/ 1 pint/$1\frac{1}{4}$ US cups, then beat in the eggs, caster (superfine) sugar and vanilla essence (extract). Strain into a medium ovenproof dish. Cook on MEDIUM for 15–18 minutes or until the custard has set. Remove from the cooker, and chill.

Sift the brown sugar over the top in an even layer. Put under a pre-heated very hot grill (broiler) to caramelize the sugar. Chill again.

To serve, tap the caramel with a spoon to break the surface.

RUM AND COFFEE PUDDING

Metric/imperial		American
75g/3 oz	butter	6 tablespoons
75g/3 oz	caster (superfine) sugar	6 tablespoons
	2 eggs, beaten	
75g/3 oz	self-raising (rising) flour	$\frac{3}{4}$ cup
	a pinch of salt	
150ml/$\frac{1}{4}$ pint	strong black coffee, cold	$\frac{2}{3}$ cup
	rum	
	DECORATION whipped cream	
	chopped nuts	

Grease a small pudding basin (mold) lightly. Cream the butter and sugar together, beating in the eggs gradually. Mix well. Fold in the sifted flour and salt carefully. Pour the mixture into the greased basin (mold). Cook, covered, for 4 minutes on HIGH. Leave to stand in the basin (mold).

Mix the coffee with rum to taste. Pour over the pudding, and leave to soak for 1 hour. Turn out, and cover with the whipped cream. Decorate with a few chopped nuts.

FRENCH CREAM RICE

Metric/imperial		American
600ml/1 pint	milk	2$\frac{1}{2}$ cups
	1 small stick of cinnamon	
	pared rind of 1 lemon	
40g/1$\frac{1}{2}$ oz	short-grain rice	3 tablespoons
60g/2$\frac{1}{2}$ oz	lemon jelly cubes (lemon gelatin dessert)	1 × 3 oz package
	water	
15g/$\frac{1}{2}$ oz	gelatine (unflavoured gelatin)	2 envelopes
150ml/$\frac{1}{4}$ pint	double (heavy) cream	$\frac{2}{3}$ cup
25g/1 oz	caster (superfine) sugar	2 tablespoons

Heat the milk with the cinnamon and lemon rind in a medium casserole for 7 minutes on HIGH. Stir in the rice, and cook on MEDIUM for 35–45 minutes or until it is cooked. Leave to cool.

Heat the jelly cubes (lemon gelatin dessert) with 200ml/ 7 fl oz/scant 1 US cup water for 2 minutes on HIGH, and stir well. Pour into the base of a 17.5cm/7 inch diameter charlotte mould or cake tin, and leave to set.

Heat 3 × 15ml spoons/3 tablespoons water in a small dish for 2 minutes on HIGH. Sprinkle on the gelatine, and stir well to dissolve.

Whip the cream lightly, then stir into the rice mixture with the sugar and gelatine, and allow to cool slightly. Pour on to the jelly in the mould, and chill before turning out.

Chocolate Butterscotch Sauce

Metric/imperial		American
1×15ml spoon/ 1 tablespoon	cornflour (cornstarch)	1 tablespoon
1×15ml spoon/ 1 tablespoon	cocoa powder	1 tablespoon
225g/8 oz	soft brown sugar	1 cup
150ml/¼ pint	milk	⅔ cup
2×15ml spoons/ 2 tablespoons	golden (corn) syrup	2 tablespoons
	a good pinch of salt	
50g/2 oz	butter	½ stick

Mix the cornflour (cornstarch), cocoa powder and sugar in a medium casserole with a little of the milk to form a smooth paste. Stir in the remaining milk, the syrup and salt. Add the butter, and cook for 5 minutes on HIGH, stirring every 2 minutes until the sauce has thickened and the sugar has dissolved. Stir again upon removal from the cooker. Serve warm or cold, with ice cream or other desserts.

Note   Although this sauce is definitely not for the figure-conscious, it is delicious and keeps well in a refrigerator for several days.

Egg Custard Sauce

Metric/imperial		American
300ml/½ pint	milk	1¼ cups
1×5ml spoon/ 1 teaspoon	lemon rind, grated	1 teaspoon
1×15ml spoon/ 1 tablespoon	cornflour (cornstarch)	1 tablespoon
2× size 2	eggs	2 large
1×15ml spoon/ 1 tablespoon	caster (superfine) sugar	1 tablespoon

Put the milk in a jug with the lemon rind, and heat for 1½ minutes on HIGH. Mix the cornflour (cornstarch) to a smooth paste with a little water. Whisk the eggs with the sugar, then whisk in the cornflour (cornstarch) paste. Remove the milk from the cooker, and whisk it into the egg mixture. Cook on MEDIUM for 6–8 minutes or until thickened, whisking lightly every 2 minutes. Stir again upon removal from the cooker.

Tea-time

Cakes and breads cooked in the microwave cooker are quick to make. The texture, flavour and colour are, however, different from those conventionally cooked, so do not make comparisons. The colour of ingredients for brown breads and tea breads is darker, while sponge cakes, which are particularly light and airy, are pale cream in colour unless cocoa powder or plain (semi-sweet) chocolate is added.

For successful cakes, avoid overbeating the mixture. Before adding dry ingredients such as flour or ground almonds, make sure they are well sifted so that there are no lumps, as these would appear in the cake. Level the surface before putting the cake into the cooker. If using packet (packaged) cake mixes, always add twenty-five per cent extra fluid to the mixture than that stated by the manufacturer unless there are specific microwave instructions which indicate otherwise.

If you have difficulty in cooking the centre of the cake, lay a sheet of greaseproof (waxed) paper over the dish for part of the cooking time. This will help to cook the centre.

Praline, toasted coconut or browned almonds all give a cake an attractive appearance, and are quick to prepare in the cooker.

Generally, cakes will not keep so long if they have been cooked in a microwave cooker. If the cake is to be used the following day, store in an airtight container.

Cooking Containers for Cakes

Use round, oblong or square dishes with rounded corners at the base. Grease the dish sparingly, and line the base with greased greaseproof (waxed) paper or layering tissue (tissue paper). Do not flour the cooking container as this would stick to the cake. Ring moulds can be greased lightly and sprinkled with caster (superfine) sugar to ensure that the cake will turn out. Leave the cake to stand for 5 minutes or more before turning out on to the serving plate.

Chocolate Fudge Cake

Metric/imperial		American
175g/6 oz	butter	1½ sticks
175g/6 oz	soft brown sugar	¾ cup
3 eggs, beaten		
100g/4 oz	self-raising (rising) flour, sifted	1 cup
50g/2 oz	ground almonds	½ cup
1½ × 5ml spoons/ 1½ teaspoons	baking powder	1½ teaspoons
100g/4 oz	plain (semi-sweet) chocolate	4 squares
FILLING AND DECORATION		
strawberry jam		
175g/6 oz	plain (semi-sweet) chocolate	6 squares

Grease a shallow 22.5cm/9 inch microwave casserole, and line the base with greased greaseproof (waxed) paper.

Cream the butter and sugar until light and fluffy. Beat in the eggs gradually. Fold in the flour, almonds and baking powder. Heat the chocolate for 5 minutes on MEDIUM, and pour into the mixture. Mix gently to distribute evenly, then put into the casserole. Cook for 12 minutes on MEDIUM, and then on HIGH for 3–4 minutes or until the cake is just coming away from the edges of the dish. Leave for 5 minutes before turning out.

When cool, slice in half, and fill with strawberry jam.

To make the decoration, melt the remaining chocolate in a small bowl for 5–7 minutes on MEDIUM, stirring every 2 minutes until smooth. Pour over the cake, and spread evenly with a palette knife (metal spatula).

APPLE WALNUT TEA BREAD

Metric/imperial		American
75g/3 oz	butter	6 tablespoons
150g/5 oz	soft brown sugar	$\frac{2}{3}$ cup
	2 eggs	
200g/7 oz	plain (all-purpose) flour	$1\frac{3}{4}$ cups
1×15ml spoon/ 1 tablespoon	baking powder	1 tablespoon
1×2.5ml spoon/ $\frac{1}{2}$ teaspoon	ground cinnamon	$\frac{1}{2}$ teaspoon
1×2.5ml spoon/ $\frac{1}{2}$ teaspoon	salt	$\frac{1}{2}$ teaspoon
2×15ml spoons/ 2 tablespoons	milk	2 tablespoons
75g/3 oz	walnuts, chopped	$\frac{3}{4}$ cup
	1 large cooking apple, peeled, cored and diced	
	ICING	
50g/2 oz	icing (confectioner's) sugar	$\frac{1}{2}$ cup
2×5ml spoons/ 2 teaspoons	cold water	2 teaspoons
	halved walnuts	

Grease a 900g/2 lb microwave loaf dish, and line the base with greased greaseproof (waxed) paper.

Cream the butter and sugar until fluffy. Beat in the eggs gradually. Sift the dry ingredients together, and fold into the mixture. Add the milk, then the nuts and apple. Turn into the loaf dish, and level the surface. Cook for 10 minutes on MEDIUM, then on HIGH for 5 minutes or until the centre is cooked. Leave to stand for 5 minutes before turning out.

Mix together the sugar and water, and then beat well. Pour over the cooled bread, and decorate with halved walnuts.

GRANARY BREAD

Metric/imperial		American
300ml/$\frac{1}{2}$ pint	water	$1\frac{1}{4}$ cups
1×5ml spoon/ 1 teaspoon	caster (superfine) sugar	1 teaspoon
2×5ml spoons/ 2 teaspoons	dried (active dry) yeast	2 teaspoons
450g/1 lb	granary (stoneground wholewheat) flour	4 cups
1×2.5ml spoon/ $\frac{1}{2}$ teaspoon	salt	$\frac{1}{2}$ teaspoon
25g/1 oz	butter	2 tablespoons
	cooking oil	
	DECORATION granary (stoneground wholewheat) flour	

Heat the water in a jug (measuring cup) for 1 minute on HIGH, then mix with the sugar and yeast. Stand for 10 minutes until frothy.

Mix together the flour and salt. Rub in the butter, and work in the yeast and water mixture gradually to form a smooth dough. Knead on a floured surface for 5–10 minutes until smooth and elastic. Put into a greased bowl, cover and leave to rise until the mixture has doubled.

Re-knead the dough, shape and put in a lightly greased 900g/2 lb loaf dish. Put inside a plastic bag until the dough is well risen.

Remove the risen dough from the bag, and brush lightly with oil. Sprinkle with a little granary (wholewheat) flour. Cook for 7–8 minutes on HIGH. Turn out, and cool on a wire rack.

Note The rising times for the dough can be limited to about 1 hour in a warm room.

COCONUT CRUNCH

Metric/imperial		American
175g/6 oz	margarine	1½ sticks
50g/2 oz	cornflakes	2 cups
1×15ml spoon/ 1 tablespoon	cocoa powder, sifted	1 tablespoon
60g/2½ oz	desiccated (flaked) coconut	¾ cup
100g/4 oz	caster (superfine) sugar	½ cup
150g/5 oz	self-raising (rising) flour, sifted	1¼ cups
	DECORATION	
100g/4 oz	plain (semi-sweet) chocolate	4 squares

Melt the margarine in a small bowl on HIGH for 1¼ minutes or until melted. Stir in the cornflakes, cocoa powder, coconut and sugar. Fold in the flour. Turn the mixture into a greased 20cm/ 8 inch flan dish (tart pan), level the surface, and cook for 4 minutes on HIGH. Mark into triangles while hot. Leave in the flan dish (tart pan) to cool.

Melt the chocolate in a small bowl for 2 minutes on MEDIUM, stirring until smooth. Turn out the triangles, and cut out. Drizzle with the chocolate.

TRUFFLE CAKES

Metric/imperial		American
225g/8 oz	plain (semi-sweet) chocolate, broken into pieces	8 squares
50g/2 oz	cake crumbs	1 cup
50g/2 oz	digestive biscuits (graham crackers), crushed	⅔ cup
25g/1 oz	sultanas (golden raisins)	2½ tablespoons
2×15ml spoons/ 2 tablespoons	apricot jam	2 tablespoons
1×15ml spoon/ 1 tablespoon	brandy	1 tablespoon

Melt the chocolate in a small bowl for 7–8 minutes on MEDIUM, stirring every 2 minutes. Use a pastry brush to coat the insides of eight fairy (cup) cake paper cases with half the melted chocolate, and chill in a refrigerator until set. Re-melt the remaining chocolate for 3–4 minutes on MEDIUM, then add a second layer. Chill in a refrigerator for several hours.

Mix together the cake and biscuit (cracker) crumbs. Add the sultanas (golden raisins), then bind together with the jam and brandy. Carefully peel the paper from the chocolate cases, and arrange them on a plate. Fill with the mixture.

Mocha Gâteau

Metric/imperial		American
100g/4 oz	plain (semi-sweet) chocolate	4 squares
6×15ml spoons/ 6 tablespoons	strong black coffee	6 tablespoons
175g/6 oz	margarine	1½ sticks
175g/6 oz	soft brown sugar	¾ cup
	2 eggs	
250g/9 oz	self-raising (rising) flour	2¼ cups
PRALINE		
75g/3 oz	granulated sugar	6 tablespoons
4×15ml spoons/ 4 tablespoons	water	¼ cup
50g/2 oz	almonds, browned and chopped	½ cup
	a pinch of cream of tartar	
ICING (FROSTING)		
100g/4 oz	butter	1 stick
225g/8 oz	icing (confectioner's) sugar	2 cups
2×15ml spoons/ 2 tablespoons	milk	2 tablespoons

Grease a 20cm/8 inch diameter deep dish lightly, and line the base with layering tissue (tissue paper) or greased greaseproof (waxed) paper.

Heat the chocolate and coffee in a jug (measuring cup) for 2 minutes on MEDIUM. Cream the margarine with the sugar, and beat in the eggs gradually. Fold in the coffee mixture and the flour alternately. Spread this mixture out in the cake dish. Cook for 12 minutes on MEDIUM, then for 2–3 minutes on HIGH until the surface is just dry. Leave to stand for 5 minutes before turning out.

To make the praline, put the sugar and water into a small bowl, and heat for 5 minutes on MEDIUM. Stir to dissolve the sugar, then heat on HIGH for 5 minutes or until the liquid turns golden-brown. Use oven gloves to remove from the cooker. Stir in the almonds and cream of tartar. Pour into a greased Swiss roll tin (jelly roll pan), and leave to cool. Crush the praline finely, or grind in a food processor.

To make the icing (frosting), cream together the butter and icing (confectioner's) sugar, and beat in the milk. Add half the praline mixture to the butter icing (frosting), and mix well.

Split the cake in half horizontally, and spread thinly with a little of the butter icing (frosting). Spread more icing (frosting) around the edges of the cake, and then roll the side of the cake in the remaining praline mixture. Decorate the top of the cake with the remaining icing (frosting).

Mocha Gâteau, Apple Walnut Tea Bread (page 66), Truffle Cakes (page 67) **and** Coconut Crunch (page 67)

Drinks

What could be better on a cold day than thawing out with a steaming hot drink, and, moreover, one that has been prepared without using a saucepan. Drinks can be made in a microwave cooker either individually in a serving mug or cup, or, for larger quantities, in a jug (measuring cup).

A cold cup of tea or coffee can be quickly refreshed on HIGH in a microwave cooker without tasting stewed.

Use the following chart as a guide to re-heating liquids.

Liquids Heating Chart

Number of servings (150ml/¼ pint/⅔ US cup per serving)	Liquid	Time on HIGH
1	Water	1½–2 minutes
2	Water	2½–3 minutes
4 (see **Note**)	Water	5–6 minutes
1	Milk	1½–1¾ minutes
2	Milk	2–2½ minutes
4 (see **Note**)	Milk	4½–5 minutes

Note Combine the total quantity of liquid in a jug (measuring cup).

Blackjack

Metric/imperial		American
600ml/1 pint	strong black coffee	2½ cups
2×15ml spoons/ 2 tablespoons	sugar	2 tablespoons
	a pinch of ground cinnamon	
150ml/¼ pint	double (heavy) cream	⅔ cup
2×15ml spoons/ 2 tablespoons	white rum	2 tablespoons
	DECORATION powdered drinking chocolate (sweetened cocoa mix)	

Mix together the coffee, sugar and cinnamon in a jug (measuring cup), then heat on HIGH for 5–6 minutes or until the liquid is very hot. Remove from the cooker.

Whip the cream until semi-stiff. Stir the rum into the coffee, then pour into four individual glasses, and top with the cream. Sprinkle each glass with a pinch of powdered drinking chocolate (sweetened cocoa mix).

VEGETABLE DRINK

Metric/imperial		American
600ml/1 pint	canned **or** bottled vegetable juice	2½ cups
2×5ml spoons/ 2 teaspoons	lemon juice	2 teaspoons
1×5ml spoon/ 1 teaspoon	Worcestershire sauce	1 teaspoon

Combine the vegetable juice, lemon juice and Worcestershire sauce in a jug (measuring cup). Heat for 5–6 minutes on HIGH until hot. Stir once during the cycle and on removal from the cooker. Pour into mugs, and serve.

MULLED CIDER

Metric/imperial		American
1 litre/1¾ pints	cider	4½ cups
2×15ml spoons/ 2 tablespoons	honey	2 tablespoons
	a stick of cinnamon	
	4 cloves	
	4 allspice berries	
	1 orange, sliced	
	1 apple, peeled, cored and quartered	

Put all the ingredients in a large container. Heat for 15 minutes on HIGH, then stir on removal from the cooker. Strain the liquid through a sieve. Decorate, if liked, with the orange slices.

EGG NOG

Serves 3–4

Metric/imperial		American
450ml/¾ pint	milk	2 cups
2×15ml spoons/ 2 tablespoons	whisky	2 tablespoons
40g/1½ oz	caster (superfine) sugar	3 tablespoons
	2 eggs, separated	
1×5ml spoon/ 1 teaspoon	grated nutmeg	1 teaspoon

Put the milk, whisky and sugar in a jug (measuring cup). Heat for 5–6 minutes on HIGH, stirring half-way through the cooking cycle.

Whisk the egg whites until light and frothy. Beat the egg yolks together lightly, and work in the hot milk mixture gradually. Stir in the egg whites thoroughly. Pour into 3–4 glasses, and serve sprinkled with grated nutmeg.

HOT SANGRIA

Metric/imperial		American
1 litre/1¾ pints	red wine	4½ cups
600ml/1 pint	water	2½ cups
	a stick of cinnamon	
	thinly pared rinds of 1 orange and 1 lemon	
	sugar	

Put the wine, water, cinnamon, and orange and lemon rinds in a large container, and sweeten to taste. Heat for 12–15 minutes on HIGH, then stir on removal from the cooker. Strain before serving.

Note This makes a light and refreshing party drink.

Variation

For a stronger version, add 50ml/2 fl oz/¼ US cup brandy before serving.

HOT APPLE AND RUM

Serves 1

Metric/imperial		American
175ml/6 fl oz	apple juice	¾ cup
1×15ml spoon/ 1 tablespoon	brown sugar	1 tablespoon
1×15ml spoon/ 1 tablespoon	rum	1 tablespoon
1×5ml spoon/ 1 teaspoon	butter (optional)	1 teaspoon

Put the apple juice and sugar into a mug or similar container, and heat for 1¾ minutes on HIGH. On removal from the cooker, stir in the rum, and top with the butter, if liked. Drink while hot.

MIXED FRUIT COOLER

Metric/imperial		American
225g/8 oz	mixed dried fruit	1¾ cups
600ml/1 pint	water	2½ cups
50g/2 oz (approx)	granulated sugar	¼ cup
	strained juice and grated rind of 1 lemon	
	ice cubes	

Put the dried fruit and water into a medium casserole. Heat, covered, for 6 minutes on HIGH. Stir in the sugar and lemon rind, and heat for 8 minutes on HIGH. Stand, covered, for 30 minutes to finish cooking.

Stir in the lemon juice, and mash the fruit lightly. Leave to stand, covered, until cold.

Strain the liquid through a sieve, pressing the fruit lightly, then chill. Serve in glasses with ice cubes in each one.

Variation

Substitute different dried fruits.

Hot Sangria, Hot Apple and Rum **and** Mixed Fruit Cooler

SWEETS (CANDIES) AND PRESERVES

The immense satisfaction derived from making home-made sweets (candies) and preserves is doubled when they are prepared in a microwave cooker as there are no dirty, sticky pans and far less chance of mixtures burning.

Jams and jellies, however, still have to be tested. Put a small amount on to a saucer, allow to cool, and see if it wrinkles when touched with a finger. Do not use a sugar thermometer in the microwave cooker as this may cause damage.

Always use a cooking container of at least 3.6 litres/6 pints/ 3 US quarts. Jams and jellies tend to rise rapidly in the container while cooking.

Do not increase the quantities of the ingredients given in the recipes as this would cause the liquid to overflow. Keep a careful eye on the recipe during cooking, and check frequently for setting point.

Jam making is particularly successful with small quantities of frozen fruit. Do not use fresh fruit when frozen is indicated.

COCONUT ICE

Metric/imperial		American
150ml/¼ pint	milk	⅔ cup
450g/1 lb	caster (superfine) sugar	2 cups
175g/6 oz	desiccated (flaked) coconut	2 cups
	red food colouring	

Combine the milk and sugar in a large container, and cook for 9 minutes on HIGH, stirring every 2 minutes. Stir in the coconut. Pour half the mixture into a greased 17.5cm/7 inch tin (pan). Mix the food colouring with the remaining coconut mixture to make it pink, and pour this on to the top. Mark into 2.5cm/ 1 inch squares, and leave to set. When cold, cut into squares.

LIQUEUR FRUIT JELLIES

Metric/imperial		American
150ml/¼ pint	white **or** red grape juice	⅔ cup
75g/3 oz	caster (superfine) sugar	6 tablespoons
3×15ml spoons/ 3 tablespoons	liquid glucose	3 tablespoons
25g/1 oz	powdered (unflavored) gelatine	3 envelopes
4×15ml spoons/ 4 tablespoons	water	¼ cup
1×15ml spoon/ 1 tablespoon	liqueur	1 tablespoon
	assorted food colourings	

Heat the grape juice, sugar and glucose in a large casserole for 6 minutes on MEDIUM. Stir to ensure that all the sugar is dissolved. Sprinkle the gelatine on to the water, and heat for 2 minutes on MEDIUM. Stir well to ensure that all the gelatine is dissolved. Stir into the grape juice, and leave to cool.

Add the liqueur and colouring, and pour into a wetted 15cm/6 inch square tin (pan). Leave to set in a cool place.

When firm, turn out, and cut the jellies into assorted shapes with biscuit cutters.

Note These jellies make a sparkling centre piece on the dining table, and can be served with coffee after dinner.

They can be stored in an airtight tin for up to 1 week.

Damson (Plum) and Pear Jam

Yield 900g–1.1kg/2–2½ lb

Metric/imperial		American
450g/1 lb	damsons (plums), frozen	1 lb
300ml/½ pint	water	1¼ cups
225g/8 oz	pears, peeled, cored and chopped	½ lb
675g/1½ lb	granulated sugar	3 cups

Put the damsons (plums) in a large container and heat, covered, for 10 minutes on DEFROST, stirring the fruit after 5 minutes. Add the water and pears. Cook, covered, for 20 minutes on HIGH. Add the sugar, and stir well to dissolve. Heat, uncovered, for 3–4 minutes on HIGH. Stir, and continue cooking, uncovered, for approximately 10 minutes on HIGH until a set is obtained. Remove the stones (pits), which will have floated to the surface, and pour the jam into hot sterilized jars. Cover with airtight seals.

Mint and Apple Jelly

Yield 900g/2 lb (approx)

Metric/imperial		American
900g/2 lb	cooking apples	2 lb
900ml/1½ pints	cold water	3¾ cups
	a small bunch of mint	
550g/1¼ lb (approx)	sugar	2½ cups (approx)
3–4×15ml spoons/3–4 tablespoons	chopped mint	3–4 tablespoons

Cut up the apples, discarding any bruised parts. Put into a large container with the water and the bunch of mint. Cook, covered, on HIGH for 25 minutes or until the apples are very soft. Mash with a wooden spoon. Leave overnight to strain though a jelly bag.

Measure the liquid, and add 450g/1 lb/2 US cups sugar for each 600ml/1 pint/2½ US cups liquid. Add the sugar to the container with the liquid, and heat, uncovered, for 10 minutes on HIGH. Stir well to ensure that all the sugar is dissolved. Heat, uncovered, on HIGH for 20–22 minutes until setting point is reached, stirring occasionally. Remove any scum. Add the chopped mint, then pour into hot, sterilized jars, and cover with airtight seals.

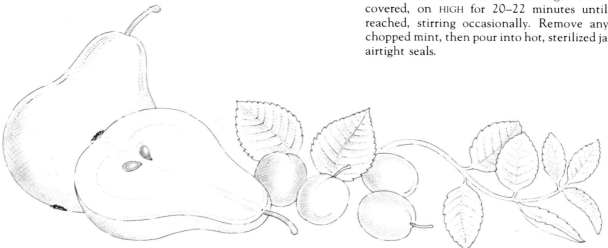

CHOCOLATE FRUIT CLUSTERS

Makes 16 (approx)

Metric/imperial		American
175g/6 oz	plain (semi-sweet) chocolate	6 squares
25g/1 oz	butter	2 tablespoons
25g/1 oz	stem (preserved) ginger (in sugar syrup), drained and chopped	2 tablespooons
25g/1 oz	cashew nuts, chopped	$\frac{1}{4}$ cup
25g/1 oz	tenderized (dried) apricots, chopped	3 tablespoons
25g/1 oz	dates, chopped	3 tablespoons
50g/2 oz	sultanas (golden raisins)	$\frac{1}{3}$ cup

Heat the chocolate and butter in a medium bowl for 3 minutes on HIGH. Remove from the cooker. Stir in the remaining ingredients, and coat thoroughly with the chocolate mixture. Drop teaspoonfuls of the mixture on to a greased tray (baking sheet) or into sweet (paper candy) cases. Chill in a refrigerator.

Variation
Add a teaspoon of a favourite liqueur to the chocolate for an extra special flavour.

HONEY WALNUT BRITTLE

Metric/imperial		American
225g/8 oz	caster (superfine) sugar	1 cup
6×15ml spoons/ 6 tablespoons	clear honey	6 tablespoons
175g/6 oz	walnuts, roughly chopped	1$\frac{1}{2}$ cups
15g/$\frac{1}{2}$ oz	butter	1 tablespoon
1×5ml spoon/ 1 teaspoon	baking powder	1 teaspoon

Put the sugar and honey into a large casserole, and cook for 6–8 minutes on MEDIUM, stirring after 4 minutes and on removal to ensure that the sugar is thoroughly dissolved. Add the nuts, and stir. Cook on HIGH for 5–7 minutes or until the syrup becomes golden. Add the butter, and cook for a further minute on HIGH, then remove from the cooker. Stir in the baking powder until the mixture begins to foam. Pour into a 20×30cm/8×12 inch lightly greased metal tray (baking sheet), and leave until cold, then break into pieces.

Chocolate Fruit Clusters, Honey Walnut Brittle **and** Liqueur Fruit Jellies (page 74)

LET'S PUT IT ALL TOGETHER

After you have practised using the microwave cooker for a few recipes and for the cooking of vegetables, you will be ready to cook a complete meal. When planning the menu, choose dishes that will not all need last minute cooking. For instance, cook a dessert or first course earlier in the day that can be re-heated just before eating, or choose one that is served cold.

Baked (jacket) potatoes, joints (roasts) and casseroles will all stand for 15–20 minutes without any rapid cooling. Even vegetables, sauces, meat in sauce and most puddings will not get as cool as when conventionally cooked. This standing time helps with the menu planning–foods that have a long standing time are cooked first. Remember also that you can open the cooker door at any time to take out one dish, put in another and then return the first. The original dish will not be affected.

Cook dishes containing shellfish, fish, cheese or eggs at the last minute, as all of these can overcook during re-heating. Equally, breads, rolls, little savoury snacks on toast and biscuits (cookies) should all be heated at the last minute.

It is well worth writing down the menu and preparation order for the first few menus you try. Ensure that any frozen food is completely defrosted before cooking, so defrost well in advance.

Use conventional equipment like a heated trolley, tray or warming oven if necessary, until you get used to the speed and retaining heat that the cooker produces.

MENU FOR 2 PERSONS

Bacon wrapped Corn-on-the-Cob (page 20)

Plaice (Flounder) in Cheese and Prawn (Shrimp) Sauce (page 38)

Broccoli Amandine (page 51)

Summer Fluff (page 56)

Earlier in the day

Soak the fruit in the wine and sugar for the Summer Fluff.
Cook 225g/8 oz broccoli for 8 minutes on HIGH. Leave to stand, covered.
Cook half the topping for the broccoli recipe for 2–4 minutes. Add to the broccoli, and leave, covered.

30 minutes before serving

Prepare the fish fillets.
Make the Cheese and Prawn sauce. Pour it over the fish, and leave to stand, covered.
Prepare and cook the Bacon wrapped Corn-on-the-Cob.
Whisk the egg white for the Summer Fluff, fold in the sugar, and cover the bowl lightly with clingfilm.

Just before eating

Cook the fish while eating the corn-on-the-cob.
Re-heat the broccoli for 3 minutes on HIGH while clearing the table.
Finish off the Summer Fluff, and serve immediately.

Vegetarian Menu

Corn and Pepper Soup (page 20)

Stuffed Aubergines (Eggplants) (page 47)

French Style Petits Pois (page 51)

Baked Bananas (page 55)

Earlier in the day

Make the soup, doubling the quantities and adding fifty per cent to all timings. Leave to stand, covered.

40 minutes before serving

Cook the peas, and leave to stand, covered.
Prepare and cook the Stuffed Aubergines.
Prepare the Baked Bananas.
Re-heat the Corn and Pepper Soup for 6–8 minutes on HIGH, and serve.
Re-heat the aubergines for 5 minutes on HIGH while eating the soup.
Re-heat the peas for 3 minutes on HIGH while clearing the table.
Cook the bananas while eating the main course.

Entertaining

Baby Onions in Wine (page 19)

Duck with Honey and Chestnuts (page 34)

French Style Petits Pois (page 51)

Baby New Potatoes (page 50)

Stuffed Peaches (page 59)

Earlier in the day

Prepare and cook the Stuffed Peaches.
Prepare and cook the Baby Onions in Wine.
Cook and peel the chestnuts for the duck.

1¼ hours before serving

Cook the duck and leave to stand, covered in foil.
Cook the peas, stopping just before the second timing.
Cook the potatoes. Drain, and leave in a covered dish.

Just before eating

Re-heat the onions for 5 minutes on HIGH, and serve.
Finish the peas while eating the onions.
Re-heat the duck for 5 minutes on HIGH while clearing the table.
Re-heat the potatoes on HIGH for 2 minutes.
Serve the main course with the potatoes.
Re-heat the peaches for 3 minutes on HIGH while clearing the main course.

INDEX OF RECIPES